The Logic of Hegel's *Logic*

The Logic of Hegel's *Logic*
An Introduction

John W. Burbidge

broadview press

LIBRARY AND ARCHIVES CANADA CATALOGUING IN PUBLICATION

Burbidge, John, 1936-
The logic of Hegel's logic: an introduction / John W. Burbidge.

Includes bibliographical references and index.
ISBN 1-55111-633-2

1. Hegel, Georg Wilhelm Friedrich, 1770-1831.Wissenschaft der Logik.
2. Logic. I. Title.

B2949.L8B86 2006   160   C2006-901078-1

Broadview Press is an independent, international publishing house, incorporated in 1985. Broadview believes in shared ownership, both with its employees and with the general public; since the year 2000 Broadview shares have traded publicly on the Toronto Venture Exchange under the symbol BDP.

We welcome comments and suggestions regarding any aspect of our publications—please feel free to contact us at the addresses below or at broadview@broadviewpress.com.

North America
PO Box 1243, Peterborough, Ontario, Canada K9J 7H5
PO Box 1015, 3576 California Road, Orchard Park, NY, USA 14127
Tel: (705) 743-8990; Fax: (705) 743-8353
email: customerservice@broadviewpress.com

UK, Ireland, and continental Europe
NBN International, Estover Road, Plymouth, UK PL6 7PY
Tel: 44 (0) 1752 202300; Fax: 44 (0) 1752 202330
email: enquiries@nbninternational.com

Australia and New Zealand
UNIREPS, University of New South Wales
Sydney, NSW, Australia 2052
Tel: 61 2 9664 0999; Fax: 61 2 9664 5420
email: info.press@unsw.edu.au

www.broadviewpress.com

Broadview Press Ltd. gratefully acknowledges the financial support of the Government of Canada through the Book Publishing Industry Development Program for our publishing activities.

Typeset by Infoscan Collette, Quebec City
Printed in Canada

For colleagues and friends in the Hegel Society of America and the Hegel Society of Great Britain

Contents

A Note on Sources and References

This book started life as an article on Hegel's Logic, written for *Volume 3: The Rise of Modern Logic: From Leibniz to Frege* of the six-volume *Handbook of the History of Logic*, edited by Dov M. Gabbay and John Woods, and published by Elsevier of North Holland in 2004. I appreciate their permission in allowing use of that material in this much expanded version. Thanks go as well to Don LePan, Tania Therien, Barbara Conolly, Judith Earnshaw and the staff at Broadview Press who have taken Stephen Houlgate's suggestion that the article be turned into a book, and made it a reality.

Throughout this study I shall be referring to Hegel's two different versions of the *Science of Logic*. The larger one, published from 1812 to 1816, with a revised first volume published in 1832, has been translated by A.V. Miller as *Hegel's Science of Logic* (London: George Allen & Unwin; New York: Humanities, 1969). I shall refer to this as *SL*. The shorter one, which is the first third of Hegel's *Encyclopaedia of the Philosophical Sciences in Outline*, has been translated by William Wallace as *The Logic of Hegel* (Oxford: Clarendon, 1874) and revised by A.V. Miller in 1975. A second translation, by T.F. Geraets, W.A. Suchting and H.S. Harris—G.W.F. Hegel, *The Encyclopaedia Logic*—was published by the Hackett Publishing Company of Indianapolis in 1991. Since this work is composed of numbered paragraphs, I have adopted the convention of using the "§" sign to indicate the paragraph, using the short form: *EL*.

For those who would like to refer to the German original, I cite the critical edition: G.W.F. Hegel, *Gesammelte Werke* (Hamburg: Felix Meiner Verlag, 1968). There are several more accessible editions available, but it is impractical to refer to all of them; and using only one inconveniences those who possess another. I shall use *GW* to indicate this source, and shall be primarily referring to Volume 11 (The Doctrine of Being of 1812 and The Doctrine of Essence of *SL* 1813), Volume 12 (The Doctrine of the Concept of *SL* 1816), Volume 13 (*Encyclopaedia of the Philosophical Sciences* 1817), Volume 19 (*Encyclopaedia* 1827), Volume 20 (*Encyclopaedia* 1830) and Volume 21 (The Doctrine of Being of *SL* 1832). This source does not include the material from Hegel's lectures, added by his editors.

Two sets of Hegel's lectures on logic have been published in German, both in the series G.W.F. Hegel, *Vorlesungen* published by Felix Meiner, of Hamburg. Volume 10, edited by Udo Rameil and H.-C. Lucas, contains the notes made by Hegel's son, Karl, the last time the course was offered in 1831 (published in 2001). An English translation is being prepared by Clark Butler. Volume 11, edited by Karen Gloy and others, is a transcript of Hegel's Heidelberg lectures on Logic and Metaphysics from 1817 (published in 1992). I shall use *V* to refer to these as well as other volumes from this series.

All other footnote references will be given in full following standard conventions. In sum:

EL = *Encyclopaedia of the Philosophical Sciences*, Part I. The Science of Logic (1830)
GW = G.W.F. Hegel, *Gesammelte Werke* (Hamburg: Meiner, 1968-)
SL = *Hegel's Science of Logic*, translated by A.V. Miller (London: Allen & Unwin; New York: Humanities, 1969)
V =   G.W.F. Hegel, *Vorlesungen* (Hamburg: Meiner, 1983-)

PART I

Prolegomena

Chapter 1

Introduction

Confusingly, George Wilhelm Friedrich Hegel wrote two different books with the same title: *Science of Logic*. One appeared in three volumes while he was headmaster of a secondary school in Nürnberg; the second is the first third of a compendium for his lectures, called the *Encyclopaedia of the Philosophical Sciences*, and was twice revised. Yet Hegel has seldom been considered a major figure in the history of logic.

There are several reasons for this. In the first place, neither text spends much time on the terms, propositions and syllogisms that make up the bulk of standard logic textbooks. Its discussion of the formal structures of correct thinking comes only in the third of its three major divisions, and even there is soon left behind for such topics as mechanism and chemism. Even when traditional logic is considered, Hegel provides no direction concerning which forms are valid and which are not. Here we have no handbook to teach us how to argue correctly.

In the second place, the chapters range through a number of concepts that sound more like traditional metaphysics. Hegel starts with being, quality and quantity, goes on to essence, existence, actuality and causality, and concludes with teleology, life and cognition. It is not at all obvious what these terms have to do with the structure of rational discourse.

In the third place, the discussion is cloaked in a dense and obscure language that is virtually impenetrable to the uninitiated. Hegel has abandoned the traditional conventions of argument where we start from accepted premises and move on to justified conclusions. His narrative shifts from one concept to another, and the transitions are described so abstractly that it is hard to decipher what he actually has in mind. Occasionally, in introductions, notes and remarks, he relaxes into more conventional discourse, discussing the theories of his predecessors or contemporary work in mathematics, science or cultural history. But these asides do not help us much with the primary text. How can we appreciate how a concept is being applied, when we have not clearly understood it in the first place?

This may be the reason that, over time, those who continue to be interested in his thought turn to other, more accessible texts. The *Phenomenology of Spirit* explores not only the most basic forms of empirical knowledge, but also the dynamics that mould our social existence. Out of its rich soil has emerged much of recent existentialism, phenomenology, deconstruction and post-modernism, even though each new movement had as its aim the overcoming of Hegelianism. The *Philosophy of Right*, which explores the fabric of our social life from the family to the state, has been accused of justifying both absolute monarchies and Marxist revolutionary thought. At the same time it has provided resources for more sophisticated analyses of the political order. Finally, notes taken by students in Hegel's lectures have inspired those interested in the philosophy of history, the philosophy of religion and aesthetics. These edited transcriptions of the spoken word lack the abstract intensity of his written texts, and regularly offer concrete illustration. [1]

All of these parts of the Heglian corpus have some kind of connection with the details of daily life. We learn from Hegel how the conflicts and tensions that have disrupted progress are in some sense necessary, and we can see how such opposition and contradiction comes to be overcome in a more encompassing perspective. We are caught up in the excitement of our human historical experience.

The *Logic* has no such direct appeal. Its focus is abstract, handling terms that are so general they seem to carry little meaning on their own: pure being, reflection, measure, appearance, reciprocity, cognition, mechanism, essential and absolute relations, number, repulsion and attraction, judgement of necessity, syllogism of reflection …; the list appears endless. It is hard to see why such terms are important, and what one is going to gain by immersing oneself in the tortuous pathway that Hegel follows when discussing them.

Some more contemplative students have, however, found in the *Science of Logic* resources for understanding the nature of reality. They want to go behind the surface of experience to discern its ultimate significance—its metaphysical constitution, we might say. The intricate connections that bind concept to concept, they say, point toward a comprehensive, unified view of the universe, in which all things are but expressions of a single ultimate reality, called the Absolute. Hegel's dense abstractions bring with them hints of a mystical beyond that transcends the finite limitations of ordinary understanding.

---

1. Even more arcane than the *Logic*, the other parts of Hegel's *Encyclopaedia*: the *Philosophy of Nature* and *Philosophy of Subjective Spirit* have been virtually ignored by the philosophical tradition.

All of this is far from what could normally be called logic, however. There is little connection to Aristotle's *Organon*, or to the *Port Royal Logic* of Arnauld and Nicole. It is hard to see what much of this material has to do with the forms of judgement, with valid syllogisms, with modus ponens or the disjunctive syllogism. In other words, the two central parts of the Hegelian corpus seem to have received the wrong name. Even if the name has some justification (since one small section does treat the traditional forms) Hegel would have been wiser to adopt the title used for his lectures: Logic and Metaphysics.[2]

Nonetheless in this book I shall argue that Hegel has much to contribute to an understanding of logic as the science of reasoning. Hegel's professed aim was to use thought to examine its own processes. The logic, he says, is the science that studies thinking as such—not the casual "thinking" that ranges over past experience in a stream of consciousness, but the disciplined thinking that grasps the meaning of things—that "conceives concepts."[3] In the course of doing so, he intends to examine the assumptions and immediate inferences that all too often are adopted as the arsenal of reflective thinking without examination, that are assumed to be so self-evident that any reasonable person could be expected to agree. In other words, Hegel's objective is to think back over our implicit presuppositions and trace how they develop one from another; he wants to provide a systematic study of the processes that characterize all rational thought. In this work we shall suggest how he goes about this task, and what it might mean for our contemporary philosophical endeavours.

From 1812 to 1816 Hegel published the *Science of Logic*, a three-volume detailed analysis of our basic rational moves. While he interspersed his dense analysis with remarks that traced connections between fundamental concepts and more conventional disciplines—mathematics and science, the history of philosophy and religion, even ordinary experience—the crux of his argument is found in the core text: abstract, compact, and using few illustrations to ease the way for the reader. Once he moved into a secure university post at Heidelberg in 1817, he needed a more accessible handbook for his students; so he prepared what he called the *Encyclopaedia of the Philosophical Sciences*, a series of succinct paragraphs that served as

---

2. This was the title Franz Anton Good used for his transcription of his lecture notes taken in Heidelberg in the summer semester of 1817. See *Vorlesungen über Logik und Metaphysik: Heidelberg 1817, V* 11. According to Udo Rameil, it is also the title Hegel used when announcing his lectures in the university prospectus every year from the summer of 1819 until the summer of 1830. Only the final lectures in 1831 had the simple title: Logic. See Udo Rameil, "Einleitung," in G.W.F. Hegel, *Vorlesungen über die Logik: Berlin 1831, Nachgeschrieben von Karl Hegel, V* 10. For conventions used in referring to sources, see p. 9.

3. "It is essentially within this science that the subject matter of logic, namely, thinking, or more specifically *comprehensive* thinking is considered." *SL*, 43; *GW* 21: 27.

theses upon which he could expand in his lectures. While the first third of this work recapitulated the earlier three-volume *Logic*, its outline form does not capture the careful development from concept to concept found there. So to accomplish our purposes in this study we shall work from the longer text.

Before discussing Hegel's argument some background would be helpful. After sketching in a few details of his life, I shall suggest how Hegel arrived at his conception of speculative logic from the first edition of Immanuel Kant's *Critique of Pure Reason*, and from Johann Gottlieb Fichte's proposal to complete Kant's project. The project developed during his early years as a university lecturer in Jena, during which he experimented with different approaches. Then, in the *Phenomenology of Spirit*, he separated Kant's concern for epistemology from the demands of pure logic. At the same time, the *Phenomenology*'s quest for absolute knowing underlies Hegel's claim that his Logic replaces what had earlier been called metaphysics. A discussion of this work will show how the study of the way pure thought thinks can also be read as an exploration of the ultimate principles of reality.

From there we shall turn to the detailed argument of the *Science of Logic*, devoting at least one chapter to each section. This makes up the bulk of our commentary.

Once we have come to the end of our exposition of the *Logic*, we shall consider some supplementary questions: the relation between the longer and the shorter logic; the changes Hegel made when he revised both these texts for second (and in the case of the *Encyclopedia*, third) editions; how he used the *Encyclopaedia Logic* in his lectures; and how the logic relates to other philosophical disciplines that reflect on nature and human society. As a conclusion I shall discuss the way Hegelian logic developed in the Anglo-Saxon world during the nineteenth century, and some of the ways in which it is currently being interpreted.

A summary discussion such as this cannot do full justice to the detailed argument of Hegel's large and complex work. It may, however, provide a point of view from which to begin, or an outline map of the whole terrain. Ultimately the reader needs to go back to the text, read it critically, and test the positions advanced in this book, as well as the assumptions brought from previous encounters with Hegel, against the words and formulations he himself chose to use in his written text. For he was not a casual writer. He knew exactly what he wanted to say, and he selected his words carefully to say just what he intended and no more. If we are to respect his integrity, we can do no less than pay attention, and do justice, to his considered opinion, even if we then want to develop and extend his insights in other directions and in novel ways.

Chapter 2

Hegel's Life

Hegel was born in Stuttgart on August 27, 1770, the son of an administrative official in the duchy of Württemberg. A state bursary, which committed him to serving its government either in the church or in education, paid his way to the theological seminary in Tübingen where, together with the poet Friedrich Hölderlin and the philosopher Friedrich Schelling, he studied philosophy for two years and theology for three.

Not wanting to enter the bureaucracy directly, he received permission to serve as tutor for a family in the Swiss canton of Bern. Using the resources of the family library in Tschugg, he continued his study into the natural sciences, the role of religion, and the finances of Bern, following from afar philosophical developments as Johann Fichte and then his colleague Schelling pushed the conceptual revolution initiated by Immanuel Kant to its limits.

Finding himself removed from the centre of German culture, he welcomed the initiative of Hölderlin and others to find for him another post as tutor, this time in Frankfurt am Main. There he continued his writing on religion and took more interest in political questions. With the death of his father in 1799, Hegel came into a small inheritance that made possible a return to academic life. He rejoined Schelling at Jena, the university of Saxe-Weimar, which was under the oversight of the minister of culture, Johann Wolfgang von Goethe, and which was the centre of German intellectual life. He soon qualified for a junior academic post, lecturing on natural law, logic and metaphysics, mathematics, philosophy of nature and spirit, and the history of philosophy. After several attempts to produce a textbook for his courses, he turned to writing an introduction for a proposed system, which he eventually called *Phenomenology of Spirit*.

By that time the Napoleonic wars had ruined the economy of Germany in general and Saxe-Weimar in particular. In the aftermath of the battle of Jena, with very little resources, Hegel learned that his chambermaid was pregnant with his son. In desperation he appealed to the good offices of his friend Friedrich Niethammer, who found positions for him, first as editor of a newspaper in Bamberg and then as headmaster of a newly established secondary school in Nürnberg. While in Nürnberg Hegel was responsible not only for instruction in the school, teaching courses on mathematics and philosophy, but also for the physical plant. During these years, not only busy with administration, but also initiating a family life with his marriage to Marie von Tucher, he managed to complete the three books of his *Science of Logic*.

The return of peace to Europe with the fall of Napoleon freed resources for the state-run universities, and Heidelberg offered Hegel a full professorship. As a textbook for his lectures there he published an outline of his system, *Encyclopaedia of the Philosophical Sciences*, and he served as an editor of, and contributor to, the *Heidelberg Yearbook*.

In 1818 he took over the chair in philosophy at Berlin that had been vacant since Fichte's death in 1814. Hegel now discovered the financial security and recognition that he had craved for so long. Students flocked to Berlin to hear his lectures (which now included the philosophy of world history, aesthetics, and the philosophy of religion), not only from other states in disunited Germany but also from Russia, Poland, Estonia and Denmark. A second edition of his *Encyclopaedia of the Philosophical Sciences* proved to be so popular that a third edition was required within three years. He had earlier expanded its paragraphs on political philosophy into a larger compendium, the *Philosophy of Right*. When he died in November 1831 at the tail end of a cholera epidemic, he was in the midst of revising the *Science of Logic*, with the first volume already in press.

The shock of his death galvanized his students and disciples. Quickly they assembled lecture notes from their colleagues and published them, together with his written works, in a "Complete Edition through a Union of Friends of the Immortalized." Some used their positions in universities and government to show that his ideas could provide the bulwark for both church and state. Many of the younger generation, however, products of a postwar "baby boom," found themselves without prospect of employment. They began to find in Hegel's thought a critique of revealed religion and a challenge to feudal and autocratic regimes.

Gradually Hegel's influence spread beyond continental Europe. In 1844 Benjamin Jowett went to Germany from Oxford to learn about Hegelian philosophy, and on his return encouraged his students to take up its study. The failure of the Revolution of 1848 scattered German emigrants, embued with Hegelian philosophy, to the United States. One of these, Henry Brokmeyer, inspired William T. Harris and others to work through the larger *Science of Logic*. And in 1865, a Scot, J. Hutchinson Stirling, published a study of the same work, entitled *The Secret of Hegel*, with a translation of its first section, on Quality. W.T. Harris brought out a translation of the section on Reflection in 1881, and H.S. McCran did the same for the section on formal logic in Volume III.

It was, however, the shorter version from the 1830 Encyclopaedia, translated by William Wallace in 1874, which first brought the whole structure of the logic to an English-speaking audience. Despite all the attempts to bring Brokmeyer's translation to press in the nineteenth century, the first translation of the larger work was that of W.H. Johnston and L.G. Struthers in 1929. More recently (1969) Arnold Miller has produced another version, while T.F. Geraets, W.A. Suchting and H.S. Harris have retranslated the *Encyclopaedia Logic* (1991). As this is being written Cambridge University Press is commissioning new translations for all Hegel's key works.

The editors of the early Complete Edition recognized that the *Encyclopaedia* text was designed for oral elaboration in lectures. So they expanded the published version of 1830 with material gleaned from lecture notes taken by Hegel's students. Since Hegel lectured on the Logic every summer during the thirteen years he was teaching in Berlin, they selected material that seemed most appropriate to each paragraph. These "additions" (as they are called) have continued to be included in translations of that text. But only recently have we had access to single sets of lecture notes, indicating how Hegel made his transitions from stage to stage. Karen Gloy has edited Franz Anton Good's lecture notes from the summer of 1817 in Heidelberg, while Udo Rameil has done the same for those of Karl, Hegel's oldest son, from 1831. The latter edition is currently being translated into English by Clark Butler for Indiana University Press.

It is useful to have two or more translations of a text. Seldom do words carry exactly the same set of meanings in the two languages. In addition, Hegel's dense prose makes it difficult to decipher exactly what he had in mind; so that translators rely on their own intuition of what may be involved—limited as it is by their own experience and familiarity with colloquial German.[1] They can not only miss subtle nuances, but read in an interpretation that is not strictly required by the words Hegel chose.

---

1. When a group of us were translating Chapter 6 of the *Phenomenology of Spirit* (G.W.F. Hegel, *Spirit*, ed. D.E. Shannon, Indianapolis: Hackett, 2001) we frequently came upon sentences that were opaque. When we turned to our predecessors for advice, we frequently found that Jean Hyppolite, translating into French, must have been faced with the same dilemma, since he would simply take over the locutions of either J.B. Baillie (into English) or E. De Negri (into Italian) neither of which really clarified the text.

The commentary that follows is based, therefore, on the German text. Translations will not always follow the published English versions. But this will add a further dimension to the process of understanding what Hegel is about. The broader the range of readings of Hegel's argument, the better sense we can get of what he originally had in mind.

For all of the obscurity of his language, Hegel's thought has evoked passionate responses. Students who had gone to Berlin to study theology with Friedrich Schleiermacher were converted by his lectures and became committed disciples. On the other hand, the crown prince of Prussia was so suspicious of Hegel's influence that, once in power, he invited Hegel's old friend, Schelling, to refute it—lectures heard by Søren Kierkegaard, Friedrich Engels and Michael Bakunin, among others. Karl Popper dismissed Hegel as not worthy of serious consideration; yet for the young John Dewey "Hegel's synthesis of subject and object, matter and spirit, the divine and the human, was no mere intellectual formula; it operated as an immense release, a liberation."[2] So there is life in these dry bones of abstract thought—life that is either dangerous or exhilarating.

It is this thought, not the details of his personal existence, which makes Hegel of interest and worthy of detailed study. It is, then, to that thought that we shall now turn.

---

2. John Dewey, "From Absolutism to Experimentalism," in *On Experience, Nature and Freedom: Representative Selections*, ed. Richard Bernstein (Indianapolis: Bobbs-Merrill, 1960) p. 10.

Chapter 3

The Background to Hegel's *Logic*

It is difficult to compare Hegel's *Science of Logic* with any other philosophical work. Unlike earlier logics, it does not focus on how concepts can be combined in judgements, and how judgements then become components of syllogisms. Unlike earlier works in metaphysics one does not start from ultimate first principles to deduce the nature of God, the cosmos and the human soul. While "being" is the initial concept, one moves on directly to nothing, and then becoming, something and other, determination, finite and infinite. There is no immediate suggestion that we are focussing on particular kinds of entities and how they are interrelated.

Nor has it been copied in the subsequent development of philosophy. Certainly Francis Bradley and Bernard Bosanquet were inspired by Hegel to write logics,[1] yet both follow a fairly traditional pattern, starting with judgements and moving on to inference. J.M.E. McTaggart wrote both *Studies in Hegelian Dialectic* and *Studies in Hegelian Cosmology*,[2] but once again the first is concerned mainly with dialectical method, while the second talks about human immortality, the personality of the absolute and the supreme good. None of these works can compare with Hegel's abstract consideration of such things as quantity and measurement, conditioning and ground, formal and real possibility, chemism and cognition, all as components of a single systematic argument.

It would appear, then, that the *Science of Logic* emerged out of nowhere as something never again to be repeated, an enterprise whose form neither drew on the history of philosophical reflection, nor captured the imagination and enthusiasm of his successors. It is studied for whatever nuggets of wisdom it might contain, but we are at a loss to understand why it takes the shape it does.

---

1. F.H. Bradley, *The Principles of Logic*, Oxford: Clarendon Press, 1883; B. Bosanquet, *Logic: Or the Morphology of Knowledge*, Oxford: Clarendon Press, 1888.
2. Both published by Cambridge University Press, the first in 1896, the second in 1901.

A clue to the new approach Hegel took, however, can be found by looking at his immediate predecessors. His understanding of logic can be traced back to a critical move in the first edition of Immanuel Kant's *Critique of Pure Reason*.

Kant distinguishes sensible intuition—the immediate presentations of our eyes, ears, touch and introspection—from the work of understanding, where the mind takes up the givens of sense into the generalities of thought. In the one we are passive, in the other we take the initiative. Whereas sense and introspection present themselves intuitively to our minds, the understanding is discursive and uses concepts. Concepts, Kant says, are *functions* which serve to *unite* diverse representations—that is, the immediate givens of sense—under something common. "By 'function'," he says, "I mean the unity of the *act* of bringing various representations under one common representation" (my italics).[3]

To identify the most basic functions that come into play when we generate concepts Kant turns to the various forms of judgement identified in traditional logic; for a judgement couples together a subject and a predicate into a single proposition. He then suggests that one and the same function not only unites subject and predicate in a logical judgement but also unites the multiple offerings of intuition into a concept; for a function as a mental action operates in the same way irrespective of the material it operates on.[4]

Kant then goes on to distinguish two ways of bringing "representations" together. One is the act of synthesis, of holding diverse representations at the same time within a single perspective. This he attributes to the imagination. The other unites by collapsing that synthetic diversity into a single thought. It involves, one could say, grasping the relationship that connects the various items together. This integrating activity is the work of understanding.[5] On one point Kant is insistent. The uniting function of conceiving cannot be derived analytically from the content united. The spontaneous activity of understanding is brought to the content imagination collects.

---

3. *Critique of Pure Reason*, B93. My citations come from *Immanuel Kant's Critique of Pure Reason*, tr. N. Kemp Smith (London: Macmillan, 1953) p. 105.

4. This argument is found in both the first and the second edition of the *Critique* as "The Transcendental Clue to the Discovery of all pure Concepts of the Understanding, Section I: The Logical Employment of the Understanding," A67–9, B92–4. Kemp Smith, pp. 105–06.

5. While this distinction between imagination and understanding can be found in both editions at A76–9 and B102–4, it is continued into the chapter on the transcendental deduction only in the first edition. By the second edition, Kant argues that conceptual unity is the condition for synthesis. It is, however, the first version of the transcendental deduction, where imagination's synthesis provides the condition for understanding's uniting, which not only inspired the romantic interest in the role of imagination but also, I am suggesting, was significant in Hegel's thinking once he began to investigate what a science of logic would be like. He will modify it (and thereby separate himself from the romantics) by claiming that thinking itself (and not only the imagination) can generate syntheses.

While Kant concentrates on the twelve types of logical judgement and the way they reveal the fundamental categories of the understanding, Kant admits that a number of other basic categories could be derived from those twelve—his examples are "force," "action," and "passion" from causality; "presence" and "resistance" from community; "coming to be," "ceasing to be" and "change" from the categories of modality.[6] Much later, at the end of the *Critique*, he defines the metaphysics of nature as "all the principles of pure reason that are derived from mere concepts and are employed in the theoretical knowledge of all things" and the metaphysics of morals as "the principles which in an a priori fashion determine and make necessary all our actions."[7] That is to say, Kant suggests that the pure concepts of the understanding can be organized into a systematic pattern that would show the underlying structure of both the world we experience and the moral realm in which we act. Hegel, it would seem, took up this challenge in his *Science of Logic*.

There are several important points to notice in Kant's argument. First, the uniting concepts of the understanding provide the foundation for the standard types of logical judgements as much as for the organization of intuitions; they explain the structures of formal logic. Second, the unity of conceiving is to be distinguished from imagination's synthesis, which only collects diversity into a single perspective. Third, Kant himself undertook the elaboration of a priori concepts into a metaphysics: in the *Metaphysical Foundations of Natural Science* and in the *Metaphysics of Morals*.

Kant's successors were impressed and excited by the way he probed into the ground of rational thinking. Yet they found his overall theory somewhat unsatisfying. Picking out the table of judgements that happened to emerge from the history of logic as the critical clue to the basic categories of the understanding looks to be an arbitrary and contingent act. Although Kant claims that these exhausted the range of fundamental principles, he does not show why these twelve and just these twelve should be given pride of place. Nor does he argue that one can derive some from others. Further, if the understanding is active and spontaneous, in contrast to the passive receptivity of sensible intuition, what constrains thought such that it has to unite its collected content using these specific functions and no others?[8]

---

6. A82/B108, Kemp Smith, pp. 114–15.
7. A841/B869, Kemp Smith, p. 659.
8. See here Hegel's Introduction to the *Science of Logic*: "What has here been called objective logic would correspond in part to what with [Kant] is transcendental logic. He distinguishes it from what he calls general logic in this way, (α) that it treats of the concepts which refer *a priori* to *objects*, and consequently does not abstract from the whole *content* of objective cognition, or, in other words, it contains the rules of the pure thinking of an *object*, and (β) at the same time it treats of the origin of our cognition so far as this cognition cannot be ascribed to the objects." (*SL* 62; *GW*, 21: 47) He goes on to write: "But if philosophy was to make any real progress, it was necessary that the interest of thought should be drawn to a consideration of the formal side, to a consideration

It was Johann Gottlieb Fichte who, using Kant's transcendental method, suggested that the spontaneous "self-positing" activity of the I or ego— Kant's transcendental unity of apperception—not only underlies all our thinking but also constitutes the concept (or category) of reality in its action. This act then provides the conditions for a second, "oppositing" activity—defined as much by what it is against as by its spontaneous affirmation of difference; this forms the category of negation. The conflict between these two, which if taken on their own cancel each other out, destroying the unity of consciousness, requires a third spontaneous activity which limits the sphere of each prior category; with this, Fichte has Kant's category of limitation. From these three he derives the other nine categories, thus extending back into the basic twelve that kind of derivation which Kant had proposed for metaphysics in general.[9]

For Hegel and his colleague Friedrich Schelling, Fichte's analysis of conceiving is partial because it implies that concepts are only subjective— the products of our understanding.[10] If it is the ego's subjective thinking that requires reference to whatever is not-ego, then we can have no confidence that our reflective conclusions apply to the world as it really is. If we are to approach anything like the truth, thinking also needs to transcend subjectivity and become objective—able to comprehend the structure of

---

of the ego, of consciousness as such, i.e. of the abstract relation of a subjective knowing to an object, so that in this way the cognition of the *infinite form*, that is, of the concept, would be introduced. But in order that this cognition may be reached, that form has still to be relieved of the finite determinateness in which it is ego, or consciousness. The form, when thus thought out into its purity, will have within itself the capacity to *determine* itself, that is, to give itself a content, and that a *necessarily* explicated content—in the form of a system of determinations of thought" (*SL* 63; *GW* 21, 48). Thus the objective logic which completes the transcendental logic needs to be supplemented by a logic of subjectivity or of conceiving,

9. See the "Fundamental Principles of the Entire Science of Knowledge," in *Fichte: Science of Knowledge*, ed. & tr. P Heath & J. Lachs, New York: Appleton, 1970, 93–119; *Fichtes Werke*, hg. I.H. Fichte, Berlin: Gruyter, 1971, I, 91–123. Once again it is instructive to note what Hegel writes in his Introduction: "If other disciples of Kant have expressed themselves concerning the determining of the *object* by the ego in this way, that the objectifying of the ego is to be regarded as an original and necessary act of consciousness, so that in this original act there is not yet the idea of the ego itself— which would be a consciousness of that consciousness or even an objectifying of it— then this objectifying act, in its freedom from the opposition of consciousness, is nearer to what may be taken simply for *thought* as such. But this act should no longer be called consciousness; consciousness embraces within itself the opposition of the ego and its object which is not present in that original act. The name consciousness gives it a semblance of subjectivity even more than does the term *thought*, which here, however, is to be taken simply in the absolute sense as *infinite* thought untainted by the finitude of consciousness, in short, *thought as such*." SL 62–63; GW 21, 47–48.

10. Kant establishes the objectivity of the concepts in his discussion of the analogies of experience. The second analogy, in particular, argues that objective concepts are those justified by sufficient reasons. Since Fichte situates the subject's relation to the "non-I" within the self-positing of the transcendental I, he abandons the quest for objectivity entirely.

the world we experience. Adopting an approach that Kant initiated in his *Metaphysical Foundations of Natural Science*, Schelling balances transcendental idealism (as he would call his version of Fichte's philosophy) with a philosophy of nature, in which thought constructs new terms by breaking them up into their constituent parts and rearranging them in appropriate ways. These constructions are then made legitimate by proofs, in which empirical evidence is shown to embody the structures of our a priori concepts.

After Schelling left the University of Jena, Hegel took over his classes on the philosophy of nature, and began to prepare a manuscript on Logic, Metaphysics and the Philosophy of Nature which adopted Schelling's method. The Logic is primarily concerned with construction, detailing the way thought develops those connections, relations and proportions that make cognition possible. The subsequent Metaphysics starts with the laws of thought and then explores the basic structures of the soul, the world and god, the knowing self, the acting self and absolute spirit. Then, in the Philosophy of Nature Hegel constructs concepts that define the mechanical, the chemical and the organic, showing that these are in fact instantiated in our experience of the world.

Hegel left this manuscript incomplete, although marginal notes suggest that he used it later either for his lectures or for subsequent compositions. He seems to have been dissatisfied with an approach that limits the logic to the analysis of traditional operations, that develops an a priori metaphysics, and that uses construction and proof for the philosophy of nature. For the works he eventually published adopt a quite different procedure.

In the final system he starts with an introduction to his system, called the *Phenomenology of Spirit*, whose basic theme is the quest for an authoritative way of knowing. Instead of plunging directly into speculative philosophy, he shows how we move from ordinary ways of interacting with the world to one which transcends all relativism—one which is absolute.

Having established that foundation, Hegel goes on to write his logic. This follows Kant in exploring the fundamental concepts that govern all our thinking. But now, since such thinking has been shown free of partiality, it grasps not only our own thinking processes, but the principles that ultimately govern the world as well. These "metaphysical principles" are then expanded to incorporate critical features of the natural and social world in the philosophies of nature and of spirit. (The full systematic exposition of these latter disciplines never did get written; Hegel was satisfied with the summary theses he had prepared for his lectures in the *Encyclopaedia of the Philosophical Sciences*, even though he did expand and revise this text several times.)

What is the reason for this shift from the approach of Schelling? It would seem that Hegel has come to acknowledge a significant difference between the concepts of pure thought on the one hand and the natural world of space and time on the other. He was, after all, a member of several scientific societies.[11] And when looking for geological specimens in the Harz mountains he would easily discover that the world does not simply instantiate our pre-ordained thoughts. Since the world is genuinely independent of our thinking of it, then we must do three things: we must show how, through our experience of the world, our thoughts come to reflect the way the world is (the *Phenomenology*); we must examine the way thought functions on its own (the *Logic*); and we must then see what happens when thought takes account of the givens of nature and human society (the *Philosophies of Nature and Spirit*).

In this new approach, it is the *Phenomenology* which establishes the reliability of our logical endeavours. Schelling and Hegel agree that the concepts we presuppose are not simply the subjective ways we humans organize our experiences; they are to capture the metaphysical principles that underlie all reality. Rather than simply showing that experience fits our concepts through the method of construction and proof, however, Hegel wants to justify the claim that thinking grasps reality, and he does so by providing a philosophical analysis of human experience. In the next chapter we shall consider how he goes about that task.

While he was following this developmental path from the philosophy of Kant, Hegel was also becoming more sophisticated in his understanding of the way pure reason functions. For this move he found inspiration in Plato's *Parmenides*. In that dialogue the aged Parmenides takes the young Socrates through a series of dilemmas, showing that, of contrary descriptions, neither of them can legitimately be predicated of "the one." It has neither parts, nor is a whole; it is neither in another nor in itself; it is neither at rest nor in motion; it can neither be the same as another thing or even itself, nor can it be different from itself or from another; it is in neither time nor space. Such negative *reductios* are echoed in Kant's antinomies of pure reason where it is proven that (for example) the cosmos must be limited because it cannot be infinite, and that it must be infinite, because it cannot be finite. In both the *Parmenides* and Kant, the examination of a feature in isolation leads to a conclusion that affirms its opposite, while starting with its contrary other reverses the shift. In both the ancient world and in the enlightenment, such exploits of sophisticated reasoning are used

---

11. On the original title page of the *Phenomenology of Spirit*, Hegel is listed not only as a doctor and professor of the University of Jena, but also as "Assessor of the Ducal Mineralogical Society of Jena and member of other learned societies." The latter refers to his ordinary membership in the Westphalian Society for the Scientific Research of Nature (from August 1804) and his honorary membership in the Physics Society of Heidelberg (from January 1807). (See K. Rosenkranz, *G.W.F. Hegels Leben*, Berlin 1844, 220.) It is worth noting that his January 1804 election to the position of Assessor and the election to the Westphalian society both occur after Schelling's departure from Jena and about the time he began working on the 1804–1805 manuscript.

to promote skepticism—the theory that nothing at all can be known. Kant follows this tradition when he uses the antinomies to show how unreliable reason is once it abandons the anchorage of experience.

Hegel, however, suspects that something more significant is going on. For Kant and the skeptics are using reason to demonstrate its own unreliability. To solve the inevitable dilemmas, then, we need to look at what is going on in the arguments. Since the reductios are reciprocal, producing contrary results, the problem does not lie in reasoning as such but in the various starting points. Kant identifies the critical flaw in the fact that reality is attributed to appearances in the original premise of each argument; one needs to draw more careful distinctions. Plato's *Parmenides*, however, suggests that the problem is more generic; it applies to all thinking whatever. What happens, suggests Hegel, is that each premise is isolated from its context and considered on its own. The paradoxical conclusion follows from this isolation, since each concept contains in its basic sense implicit relationships with other terms; once these have been excluded from consideration the original term is no longer internally consistent. Since the same problem applies to its contrary, we can hope to resolve the dilemma by bringing the two together into a single perspective. From there we can notice what it is that triggers the two reductios. Once we grasp the total picture, and consider both contrary inferences at the same time, we see that there is an underlying significance that has been overlooked—a larger perspective in which the two original terms are not isolated units, but moments of a larger whole and, like all moments, come to be and pass away. They cannot be separated off and made permanent. This is why, for Hegel, skepticism "is itself the negative side of the cognition of the absolute, and immediately presupposes reason as the positive side."[12]

This insight enabled Hegel to make another advance on Kant. In the first edition of the first *Critique* understanding can unite a synthesis into a concept, but that synthesis is the product of imagination—the creative bringing together of a number of sensible intuitions. But the reciprocal reductios of skepticism mean that it is reason, not imagination, that brings each term together with its opposite. They implicate each other, and so the synthetic perspective is not simply imaginative but rather rational. The task of understanding is to find a way of integrating that rational double pattern into a new single concept. No longer, then, do we need to follow Kant in limiting pure thought to being the handmaid of experience and imagination; it can itself generate diversity and synthesis: an isolated concept leads over into its antithesis; a simple beginning produces diversity.

---

12. "On the Relationship of Skepticism to Philosophy," in *Between Kant and Hegel*, translated by G. di Giovanni and H.S. Harris (Albany: State University of New York Press, 1985) 323; *GW* 4: 207.23–25.

Since that antithesis leads back to the original thought, both belong to the same perspective; they are thereby brought together into a synthesis. Then understanding can integrate that synthesis into a unity—a single thought that can in its turn be isolated from its context.

A logic that derives concepts in this way certainly requires a careful, reflective isolation of various intellectual operations, noting their distinctive features, as well as a readiness to recognize both how they are derived one from another and the significance of that bond. To write about such processes of thought we must use language with care to ensure that we capture the precise meaning of each concept and of each transition. Illustrations and examples too often draw attention to incidental details (the empirical context, for example) rather than to the intellectual functions and shifts of meaning that are Hegel's primary concern. So it is not surprising that Hegel develops his argument in abstract language, where he relies not on familiar experience, but on the conceptual significance of each noun and each verb. The result is a density in Hegel's text that has always posed problems for his interpreters.

This is complicated by his focus on the discursive dynamic of reasoning, for he wants to show how terms skeptically shift in meaning as reflective thought turns its attention to their various components. Rather than relying on conventional syllogisms and arguments, he is offering an analytical description of how meanings shift and coalesce.

Yet for all the density of Hegel's writing, he is not trying to be esoteric, developing an arcane discipline, known only to initiates. By "thought" he means at the very least that "common store of thoughts" which humans have "transmitted from one generation to another."[13] "It is in human language," Hegel writes, "that the forms of thought are, in the first instance, set out and laid down." He is interested in the meanings embedded in the terms we use every day. "In everything that becomes something internal—some kind of representation—for us humans, in everything that we make into

---

13. The phrase is from G. Frege's "Sense and Reference," in *Translations from the Philosophical Writings of Gottlob Frege*, ed. P. Geach & M. Black (Oxford: Blackwell, 1966) 59. To talk about the logic as thought thinking through its own processes might appear to fall afoul of the charge of psychologism as originally made by Frege. But Frege, in making this charge, draws a distinction rather similar to the one made by Hegel between pure concepts and representations in general. "In order to be able to compare one man's mental images with another's we should have to have united them into one and the same state of consciousness, and to be sure that they had not altered in the process of transference. It is quite otherwise for thoughts; one and the same thought can be grasped by many men. The constituents of the thought and *a fortiori* things themselves, must be distinguished from the images that accompany in some minds the act of grasping the thought—images that each man forms of things." [Review of Husserl's *Philosophie der Arithmetik* in *Zeitschrift für Philosophie und phil. Kritik*, 103 (1894), 317–18;

language and then utter," he goes on to say, "there is contained a category, hidden, mixed up and articulated. That is how natural logic is for us; indeed it is our own peculiar nature."[14]

The following discussion uses as its guiding thread the principle that Hegel's abstract vocabulary names and describes the functions of pure thought hidden in our language—not only those that unite, but also those that discriminate and those that skeptically shift from one thought to its counterpart or completion. Ultimately it should be possible to make some connection from Hegel's abstract prose to our conventional meanings. That may mean ignoring certain psychological associations; it may involve distinguishing within a confused jumble several related, but distinct, senses of diverse terms; it may demand setting aside certain preconceptions until we understand more precisely what Hegel is trying to say. All of that requires strenuous intellectual effort. But the result can also be rewarding. For, by becoming more adept in our thinking, we develop control of our inner life.

---

translation from *Translations from the Philosophical Writings of Gottlob Frege*, ed. P. Geach & M. Black (Oxford: Blackwell, 1966) 79.] In "Sense and Reference" he again draws a distinction between what he calls an idea or internal image and "the sign's sense, which may be a common property of many and therefore is not a part or a mode of the individual mind. For one cannot deny that mankind has a common store of thoughts which is transmitted from one generation to another." [Ibid. 59] It is the "act of grasping the thought" or the "sign's sense," the common store "transmitted from one generation to the next," which is the focus of Hegel's attention, not the transient and idiosyncratic images that accompany them.

14. *SL 31*, *GW 21: 10*. Preface to the Second Edition. The translation is my own.

Chapter 4

Metaphysics and Hegel's *Phenomenology*

In the Introduction to his *Science of Logic* Hegel says that its first volume, the "objective" logic, takes the place of metaphysics.[1] This is a bold claim, especially in light of recent philosophical developments.

Traditionally, rationalists like Descartes and Spinoza had used pure thinking to construct a disciplined understanding of the world. The resulting thoughts were to capture what is essential about the way things are. Kant, however, had challenged this approach. Though he continued to write metaphysical works—*The Metaphysics of Morals*, for example, and *The Metaphysical Foundations of Natural Science*—he limited their application to the way we *experience* things: the concepts we must use whenever we understand the givens of sense and introspection. The world as it is in itself lies beyond human ken.

As we have seen, Hegel and his colleague Schelling challenged the subjectivism of both Kant's philosophy and its elaboration at the hands of Fichte and others. Reality is both subjective and objective. Our thoughts, they wanted to maintain, are able to grasp not simply the way *we* understand the world, but the way the world actually is. Hegel goes so far as to stress that the pure philosophical science "*contains thought to the extent that it is at the same time the heart of the matter on its own, or the heart of the matter on its own to the extent that it is pure thought.*" Indeed, he becomes quite lyrical: "The logic is therefore to be taken as the system of pure reason, as the kingdom of pure thought. *This kingdom is the truth laid bare in and of itself.* One can express it this way: that this content is the *portrayal of God as he is in his eternal essence before the creation of nature and a finite spirit.*"[2]

---

1. *SL* 63; *GW* 21: 48. Compare §24 in *EL*: "The *logic* coincides with *metaphysics*— the science of *things* grasped in *thoughts*, which in that way served to articulate what are the *essentials* about *things*."
2. *SL* 49–50; *GW* 21: 33–34. All emphasis is found in the original.

Anyone coming after Kant, however, cannot get away with simply making such assertions. For Kant we humans are essentially finite; our thoughts can never reach the world as it is in itself. We are limited to the givens of sense, filtered through our own specific locations in space and time. And Hegel is well aware of this fact. When he says that the logic is the "system of pure reason," after all, he is playing on Kantian themes. For Kant himself had said that "the philosophy of pure reason is either a *propaedeutic* (preparation), which investigates the faculty of reason in respect of all its pure *a priori* knowledge, and is entitled *criticism*, or secondly, it is the system of pure reason, that is, the science which exhibits in systematic connection the whole body (true as well as illusory) of philosophical knowledge arising out of pure reason, and which is called *metaphysics*."[3]

So Hegel is presenting himself with a dilemma. How can he at the same time pretend to be completing Kant's task in constructing a system of pure reason and yet reject Kant's fundamental division between the world of experience which we think about and the world as it is in itself that is beyond all thought?[4]

Hegel's answer to this dilemma is to be found in the introduction he wrote for his system: the *Phenomenology of Spirit*. This work defies traditional categories of philosophical literature. Since its theme is the quest for an absolute way of knowing, it would appear to be an epistemology. But in contrast to traditional epistemologies Hegel does not start from claims which cannot be doubted, constructing on this foundation a superstructure of decreasing certainty. Unlike the empiricists, he is not prepared to say that the senses give us direct access to truth; unlike the rationalists he suspects that clear and distinct ideas may be the result of particular circumstances, not direct insight into the mind of God. He takes us instead along the itinerary of a consciousness that continually makes strong claims to knowledge, only to find that when it puts those claims into practice it gets the opposite of what was intended. Such a pathway would seem to be no royal road to wisdom but rather a pilgrimage into skepticism and despair.

---

3. *Critique of Pure Reason*, A841/B869, Kemp Smith, 659.
4. In §76 of the *Critique of Judgment* Kant stresses the importance of the distinction: "It is indispensably necessary for the human understanding to distinguish between the possibility and the actuality of things. ... The whole of our distinction between the merely possible and the actual rests on this, that the former only signifies the positing of the representation of a thing in respect of our concept and, in general, in respect of the faculty of thought, while the latter signifies the positing of the thing in itself (outside of this concept)."

It is not our purpose here to provide a detailed commentary on the *Phenomenology of Spirit*. Many others have undertaken this task, and students have rich resources at their disposal.[5] The following paragraphs are designed instead to show how Hegel resolves his metaphysical dilemma in the pages of that work.

To have concepts which capture the nature of reality is to have knowledge, and when that knowledge contains no residue of partiality it is "absolute": "valid in all respects."[6] Hegel undertakes to examine the claims humans make when they are absolutely certain they know the way things are. Inevitably experience shows that the certainty is misplaced. The world seldom fits our confident expectations.

But he does more. For he orders the sequence of claims in such a way that each one rises, phoenix-like, from the ashes of the preceding. The earlier confidence is gone, but a residue remains that is built into the more complex epistemological convictions that follow. This increasing complexity means that the *Phenomenology* ranges far beyond the traditional types of epistemology. Certainly it starts from an empiricist focus on direct sensation and the way it is grasped through the medium of thought. But it moves on to consider confident claims concerning self-knowledge, to a rationalist reliance on categories common to self and world, whether physical or psychological, to convictions concerning the nature and functioning of society, and even to confident religious affirmations about the nature of ultimate reality.

At each stage a claim to knowledge is made that is to be valid in all respects. And at each stage that claim turns out to fail at the hands of experience, whether personal or social. So even though "absolute knowing" is the title of Hegel's final chapter, it is also the constant theme of the whole work. Every claim to absolute knowledge turns out to be relative and partial.

It is probably worthwhile to consider some examples of this process.

Hegel starts by considering the claim that knowledge should brook no interference from reflective thought. We know just what we sense directly. That means to say that the sounds we hear and the sights we see are true just as we see and hear them. The problem is that these sights and sounds don't stay around. At one moment we see the sun break over the eastern horizon; at another the full moon shines down from the highest heavens. In

5. H.S. Harris, *Hegel's Ladder* (Indianapolis: Hackett, 1997) provides a detailed analysis of each chapter, documenting the rich resources in the western tradition upon which Hegel draws. Other useful commentaries are: Joseph Flay, *Hegel's Quest for Certainty* (Albany: SUNY Press, 1984), Jean Hyppolite, *Genesis and Structure of Hegel's Phenomenology of Spirit*, tr. S. Cherniak & J. Heckman (Evanston: Northwestern UP, 1974), Kenneth Westphal, *Hegel's Epistemological Realism* (Dordrecht: Kluwer, 1989) and Merold Westphal, *History and Truth in Hegel's Phenomenology* (Albany: SUNY Press, 1979).

6. The phrase comes from Kant, *Critique of Pure Reason*, A324/B381, Kemp Smith, p. 317.

one place we hear a nightingale sing; somewhere else we are deafened by a tumultuous waterfall. What is true in all this sensing? Since we are to avoid any reflection, it can only be that particular sound or sight that we are immediately aware of and nothing else. But that conflicts with the initial claim, which wants to say that *whatever* we are sensing directly is true.

The one thing constant in all that variety is the fact that I am sensing it, so the next move is to say that it is this constant I which determines the truth of the experience. But it turns out that there are other egos, all of whom have their own peculiar range of sensations.

So the truth of the experience can lie neither in the particular object sensed, since it always moves, nor in the particular subject sensing, since there are many. It must lie in the immediate act of sensing itself—the simple and unaffected relationship between the sensing and the sensed.

The early simplistic claims to immediate sensation have given way to a more sophisticated one: immediate sensation is simply the direct act of sensing whenever and wherever it happens. But here experience plays its final and most devastating hand. For time passes. A sound is heard for an instant; that instant disappears into the past and the sound continues into the next. We have a new direct act of sensation, yet we want to say that we hear the same sound. In saying so we are reconstituting the buzz from the immediate past into our present and bonding the two together. We are aware of a patch of colour, but our attention moves up or down to its limit where we see a contrasting shade. Once again we take something that is past and reconnect it with our current sensation. In other words, it is impossible to ostracize completely all intervention from reflective thought. We mediate past with present, one place with another. The absolute claim of sense certainty to unmediated knowing fails.

The next move, Hegel suggests, takes up where immediate sensing left off. It is still interested in the things we sense, but it recognizes that these sensations are not unmediated—they are rather continuous stretches of experience over time and space which share a common feature. Because these stretches incorporate a number of individual sensations they are not singular, but in some sense universal. We perceive whites and browns and greens, songs and buzzes and rustlings, sweets and sours and bitters, hards and smooths and sharps. And we recognize that these perceptions are clustered into things: a smooth, green, fragrant and rustling leaf; a sweet, white, hard cube of sugar. Here the knowledge claim varies in new ways: do we know for sure the various qualities and construct the leaf or the sugar in our minds; or do we know the particular thing, and reflectively abstract out the different qualities?

Let us move on to some different sorts of claims. Certain selves claim that they really know themselves when they appropriate whatever they desire. When challenged by other selves they find that their strategy of appropriation is resisted and they no longer find straightforward satisfaction, so they try to destroy that other, discovering in the very struggle a new sense of self. If the result of the struggle is death, the vanquished dead combatant has lost all self-knowledge whatever, and the victor is left bereft of that excitement which had, for a moment, given life its meaning. So the next time a struggle occurs, and death threatens, the vanquished cries "uncle" and the victor accepts his submission.

The result is a new kind of self-knowledge—indeed two different kinds. One is independent, having his desires catered to by the other, revelling in the fawning solicitude of the slave and the luxury of all that is provided. The other is dependent, allowed to live only at the whim of the master, and forced to expend his time on producing goods for the other to enjoy. Once again, however, experience confounds the initial confidence that truth has been achieved. For the one supposed to be independent turns out to be dependent on the service provided by the other. And the dependent one, well aware that life is more important than independence, discovers that his living activity can produce the beautiful, the delectable, the effective, the impressive, and the enjoyable. Prevented from simply appropriating these products of his labour, he is able, for a moment, to contemplate them and realize that the form they have acquired is nothing but an embodiment of his living activity. He develops an independent sense of worth.

Once again, the demise of one kind of knowledge claim provides the basis for the next. For both the slave who thinks about what he has learned, and the master who recognizes how he has become dependent, divorce themselves in thought from that environment, and attribute true self knowledge to the pure thoughts one develops out of oneself. Both, then, may become Stoics.

Hegel traces the way people learn from experience through a long sequence of developments that expands to include confident societies like Greek Athens, the Roman empire, the enlightenment and the French Revolution. The story ends with a stage Hegel calls the "beautiful soul."

Conscientious individuals become disillusioned with moral principle as the proper standard for action, since it is frequently used to justify immoral action. So they appeal instead to their educated sensibility—their conscience—through which they are directly aware of what should be done in any situation. Once they act on this insight, however, their actions produce unintended results, and come to be condemned by others, equally enlightened, who have refrained from acting. Faced with this condemnation, the agent examines herself and admits failure. When the condemning judge persists in his rejection he too violates his own principles and, in renewed self-awareness, forgives the other. The result is reconciliation.

What we learn from this experience of failure brings us to what Hegel calls absolute knowing. Before making that step, however, he introduces another sequence—that of religion. Up to now we have had humans making strong claims to absolute knowledge based on their own abilities, whether in isolation or in community. In religion, believers affirm with confidence their understanding of the nature of ultimate reality. In its final stage, manifest (or revealed) religion tells a story of how the world is created out of nothing by God, how created beings fall and produce the opposite of what was intended, how God as judge becomes human to re-establish the good that was intended but is himself put to death and becomes a universal spirit, how fallen humans realize not only that they are evil in executing God, but also that there is no longer a "God-out-there"—only a spiritual presence in which they now share.

Absolute knowing, says Hegel, brings together the beautiful soul and revealed religion. The result of the condemned failure of conscientious action is not an abandonment of any such action. Rather it is the realization that all action follows the same pattern: conviction results in action; action produces unintended results that conflict with our intentions; and we then integrate those results with our earlier perspective.

This pattern is not only a truth discovered from the failure of the beautiful soul to realize its ends; it is also the recurring theme of each previous stage in the *Phenomenology.* That rhythm of confidence, action, failure and reconciliation is the central core of all human knowing and acting. But there is more, for the story told by revealed religion says that this is also the pattern of reality as a whole. It is the implicit truth of the universe, a truth affirmed by the rich accumulation of human experience over time, as well as by the insights of those religious saints who are open to the rhythms of the cosmos.

We can now see how Hegel solves the dilemma we mentioned earlier. For he has shown that our knowing is not simply subjective, as Kant had maintained. In the first place, at every stage the recalcitrance of objective fact frustrates our claims to absolute knowing. As we continue to incorporate these results into our revised claims, they become more and more comprehensive. And at the end we are saying that it is the very dynamic of learning from experience—of learning from our failures, which is the way our thinking matches the world we want to know. The surprise in Hegel's analysis is that this same pattern is ascribed to ultimate reality—explicitly in the "revelation" of Christianity, and implicitly in all other religions.

Hegel is not saying, then, that we know the truth in the sense of having insight into a lot of facts; we do not know everything. We rather know that everything we "know" will turn out to be partial and need to be incorporated into more comprehensive understanding.[7]

When Hegel comes to the *Logic,* then, he can build on the conclusions of the *Phenomenology.* Our thinking has been educated by the long experience

---

7. In Chapter 20 we shall suggest the logical pattern that provides the systematic structure of the *Phenomenology of Spirit.*

of our human species, and is characterized by the ability to learn from failure. Pure reason is thus dynamic. Each concept we focus on, while capturing a truth inherent in that experience, turns out to be partial, and comes to be a component of one more encompassing. The *Phenomenology* has taught us that this pattern is not simply a subjective feature of our reasoning. It is the distilled result of our interaction with the world throughout the long panorama of human history. So human thinking incorporates into its own functions what we have learned from putting our ideas into practice in the real world. As a result of this experiential accretion, Hegel suggests, we are not simply working in a realm far removed from the concrete realm of particulars (a charge often made of Plato's ideas); we are rather, in the *Logic*, exploring the essence of human experience as it has developed over the millennia. Into this thinking or conceiving are distilled all the forms of consciousness and their concrete experiences.[8]

This identification of thinking with the essence of human cumulative experience adds a dimension to Hegel's logic that takes him beyond Kant. For it means that the concepts pure thought thinks, as well as the transitions it makes, capture the structures and processes of reality. Traditional metaphysics had used reason to determine the nature of being per se. By showing in the *Phenomenology* that human reason has been educated over the ages by its experience of the world and society so that it has come to embody the patterns and structures of reality, Hegel can claim that what pure thought discovers as it works through its own thoughts are not only the logical principles underlying all our thinking about the world, but also the metaphysical principles which make up whatever is. His objective logic takes the place of what previously had been called metaphysics.

---

8. Again from Hegel's Introduction: "In the *Phenomenology of Spirit* I have exhibited consciousness in its movement onwards from the first immediate opposition of itself and the object to absolute knowing. The path of this movement goes through every form of the *relation of consciousness to the object* and has the concept of science for its result. The concept therefore (apart from the fact that it emerges within logic itself) needs no justification here because it has received it in that work, and it cannot be justified in any other way than by this emergence in consciousness, all the forms of which are resolved into this concept as their truth." *SL* 48 (Throughout I have altered Miller's "Notion" to "concept" to make clear the relationship to Kant); *GW* 21: 32.

PART II

The Doctrine of Being

Chapter 5

Being and Immediate Inference

If the *Science of Logic* is to be the "system of pure reason,"[1] then Hegel has to show how the basic concepts underlying all thought are related to each other in a systematic way. The first question he has to consider is where to begin; for presuppositions contained in the starting point will influence and determine the rest of the development.

In general, he says, thoughts discriminate by drawing a determinate difference between one sense and another. By finding a thought that is completely indeterminate—that can be applied to anything whatever—he can avoid introducing arbitrary distinctions. This thought, he suggests, is "being." The verb "to be" may be predicated of anything whatever without discrimination and, on its own, cannot distinguish irrational or imaginary concepts from real ones.

Pure thought finds, however, that with all this indeterminacy it is really contemplating nothing. In other words, our thinking has moved from the simple concept "being" to what one would consider its opposite: "nothing."

When we turn our attention to "nothing," we find that it, too, is completely indeterminate; yet it is being thought. So, surprisingly, it fits the same defining characteristics as "being" does. Conceiving has now moved back to the term with which it began.

Since our thinking is quite free, we can reflect back over what has happened to figure out what went on. We usually think of "being" and "nothing" as radical opposites; yet they now appear to have identical characteristics. To be identical yet opposed is contradictory, which is quite unsatisfactory. So thought must find an explanation or ground to resolve the paradox.[2]

---

1. *SL* 50; *GW* 21: 34.
2. As we shall see when we come to that logical operation, contradiction is not the end of reasoning, but rather a clue that something is wrong, pointing toward a solution that will resolve the paradox.

The two terms, "being" and "nothing," are not simply identical. In each of the two episodes we started with one and ended with the other. That is to say, with "nothing" thought has *passed over* from "being," and then with the second "being" thought has *passed over* from "nothing." This move of "passing over" is itself an activity of thought and needs to be identified. In ordinary language the term that captures its sense is "becoming."

When we look more carefully, however, we note that "becoming" is not a simple term. The movement from "being" to "nothing" is more properly called "passing away," while the move from "nothing" to "being" involves more specifically "coming to be."

At this point Hegel makes his most characteristic move. Recall that, for Kant in the first edition of the *Critique*, the *unity* of the concept is to be distinguished from the *synthesis* of the imagination, even though the latter sets the conditions for the former. In this instance it is thought, not imagination, that brings together "passing away" and "coming to be" into a synthesis. We have an infinite regress: "being" passes away into "nothing," then comes to be from "nothing," only to pass away again, and again come to be. The simple transitions of thought, by reciprocally leading into each other, have become not only a synthesis but also a self-perpetuating cycle. What now happens is that this circle collapses into a single thought—into a unity. Since it incorporates all the thinking that led up to it, it can be thought without reference to anything else; it can be considered as completely unmediated. So we have a new concept: of a kind of being that involves coming to be and passing away. For this concept Hegel adopts the German term "*Dasein*," sometimes translated "determinate being," but at this point much more indeterminate.[3]

The episode so far described can be found in the short first chapter of Hegel's *Science of Logic*. We have enough, however, to identify some important features characteristic of his method.

In the first place, Hegel takes seriously those shifts that happen in our mind when we are trying to define a concept. Usually this involves moving to those contraries that are excluded by the initial sense. So, for example, when we think "some" we immediately pass over to thinking the "other" that is excluded. In this most primitive stage of the logic, we have the realization that, in thinking the pure indeterminacy of "being," we are in fact thinking "nothing." Immediate intellectual transitions such as these are an inherent part of the meaning we are investigating, but we tend to notice them only after they have happened. And all too often we dismiss them as irrelevant to our initial task. But, says Hegel, we need to include them in our investigation of what it means to think.

---

3. One could adopt Paul Tillich's suggestion and distinguish "pure being" (in German *Sein*) from "a being" or "beings" (*Dasein*), although this does not capture the generality of the latter term.

In the second place, then, thought is able to reflect on its own processes. Not only can it take note of the fact that our thoughts have moved, but it can also look at that transition as a whole, and identify its distinctive constellation as shifting from this particular starting point to this particular terminus. In this way we can identify the conceptual sense involved in this intellectual movement. At a further level, reflection can turn its attention to a pair of moves which are reciprocal, moving back and forth from one term to its contrary, and bring them together into a synthesis. As in the case of "coming to be" and "passing away" this turns out to be an infinite cycle that can be called regressive or progressive, depending on your point of view.

In the third place, however, there is a very distinctive move, which Hegel calls (in German) *Aufhebung* and which is sometimes translated as "sublation." In this move reflection cancels its own second order status and returns us to an immediate thought. This occurs whenever we have a reciprocity that produces an unending cycle. Through sublation, thought integrates that reflective synthesis into a new unity: *Dasein*. This move is structurally identical with that function Kant identified as the work of understanding: taking a synthesis and conceiving a single, united concept. And it returns us to the direct immediacy of thinking from where we began, even though the content of our thought is now more sophisticated.

As Hegel became more aware of the dynamics of his systematic thought, he stressed the importance of what he calls the "double transition:" the reciprocal move from one thought to its opposite and back again that leads to sublation. In the second edition of his *Encyclopaedia Logic* of 1827 he adds a paragraph at the end of the *Logic* which shows how the double process cancels the one-sidedness of each of the original contraries;[4] and in the second edition of his larger *Logic* of 1831 he observes, towards the end of his discussion of Quantity, that "this remark concerning the necessity of the *double* transition is of great importance for the whole scientific method".[5] It is the double transition that generates a synthesis which (unlike in Kant's philosophy) belongs to thinking itself, not to imagination, and which thus enables pure thought to develop its concepts systematically. Sublation (or *Aufhebung*) collapses this intellectual synthesis into a new unity, so that each of the components becomes but a passing moment within a larger whole.

Hegel, however, provides a more succinct description of his method. When introducing logic to his students in his *Encyclopaedia*, he suggests that the logical has three "sides": understanding, dialectic reason and speculative

---

4. *EL* § 241 in both the second and the third edition.
5. *SL* 323; *GW* 21: 320, Hegel's emphasis.

reason.[6] Understanding isolates a concept as a unit of thought. It integrates a synthesis into a unity and marks out its determinate limits. Dialectical reason is the transition of thought that moves from a concept to its contrary. This direct shift, suggests Hegel, is the inevitable result of isolating a term from its context through understanding. Speculative reason is the work of reflection: it looks back over what has happened, sees the various moments as well as their connection, and identifies the significance of what has gone on. As we have seen when looking at what has gone on in the first chapter of the *Logic*, there are two distinct aspects of this process: first, reflection notices the transitions that connect "being" to "nothing" and vice versa; but, second, it spots how "coming to be" and "passing away" are reciprocal and mutually require each other. In this latter move speculation sets the synthetic stage for understanding to come on the scene once again with its integrating ability.

---

6. In the first edition he had this at the very beginning of his "Preliminary Conception" (*GW* 13 §§13–16). By 1827 it came after that general discussion and initiated the move into the logic proper, at *GW* 19 (and *GW* 20) §§79–82. One should compare this text with the more polemical comments concerning method to be found in the Introduction to the larger *Science of Logic*: *GW* 21: 38–41; *SL* 54–57.

Chapter 6

Quality

Determinate Being

Because it starts with "being" as the most indeterminate concept, the first chapter of Hegel's *Logic* is rudimentary and basic. As we proceed, terms become more sophisticated, but they do so only gradually and as the argument requires it. The concept which ended the first set of moves, *Dasein* (or "determinate being"), is still rather indefinite. Yet in contrast to the original concept "pure being," it contains an element of nothingness within its meaning, for it is a being that comes to be and passes away. No longer completely indeterminate, it is distinguished by that negativity. That is to say, it is qualified. We could say that the "quality" of such a being defines its reality, though at the same time (since it sets a limit to its being) it could equally well be defined as its negation.[1]

At this primitive stage, "quality" focuses on nothing more than the reality of the being that is qualified as well as negating or limiting its pure being. Such a qualified being, considered as a single unified concept, would be called "something." When we think of "something," however, we inevitably find ourselves thinking of something else, or "other"; and that shift from something to other we call "alteration," or "becoming other."

We now reflect on the two thoughts that have emerged. Both could be called "something," yet both are also "other"; so the genuinely new thought is "otherness" as such. To decipher this last concept, we must consider the two "somethings" together. On the one hand, each maintains itself as not the other. That is to say, "being-other" is a key aspect of what it is; Hegel calls this otherness, built

---

1. Hegel seems to suggest that this defining of quality as both reality and negation is a second-order judgement, using resources later defined under reflection. At this early stage, a quality is just that—a quality—and nothing more can be said. The first edition of the *Science of Logic* constructed this argument in quite a different way, making "reality" and "negation" key moments in the argument appearing at quite different stages. See Chapter 17 below.

into its being: "being-for-other." On the other hand, each has its own positive status, it is something "in itself." The concept "otherness," then, involves both "being-for-another" and "being-in-itself." And that relationship defines the way "something" is determined. So the next concept that has to be examined is "determination."

Once we think about what "determination" involves, we distinguish between the way a thing is determinate in itself, and the way it is influenced or "constituted" by something else—what we could call its "constitution." For all that we can conceptually differentiate between them, determination and constitution are closely related. For the way a thing is determined enables it to be open to the influence of another; and that influence produces changes in the original determination. As now understood, then, "something" controls its alteration; it is no longer passively affected. And what started out as its "quality" has now become the "limit" beyond which it cannot go without becoming something else entirely. We call a limited being the "finite."

With "finite" our thought has shifted once again. For the finite being continues to have its own inherent being—its "being-in-itself." But the qualitative limit becomes a "barrier," beyond which it would cease to be. Calling it a barrier, however, suggests that there is an inherent drive to go beyond that limit, something we could call an "ought."[2] Any finite being involves both a barrier and the drive beyond it.

Thought immediately moves on to whatever would be beyond the barrier. Since it is other than the finite, we could call this "beyond" the "infinite," following a tendency in much religious thinking. Unfortunately once we turn our attention to any such beyond, it becomes itself qualified and determinate, and so limited and finite. Thought thus moves from the thought of the finite, to the thought of an infinite beyond, only to have the latter become something finite in its turn, for which there is another beyond[3] ... and so one proceeds in an infinite qualitative regress.

This, however, introduces a second sense for the term "infinite." What started as simply an indefinite beyond now becomes an ongoing, repetitive process, in which the finite in general does not disappear but persists (and is to that extent infinite) and the infinite can only be defined as the opposite of some finite (and to that extent limited and finite).

Hegel has thus reached a cyclical pattern that resembles, yet is more complicated than, the reciprocal moves from "being" to "nothing" and back again. The concept "finite" leads into "infinite," and "infinite" leads back to "finite." The two moments of finite and infinite are reciprocally interconnected in a conceptual synthesis where each constitutes and requires the other. In fact this whole synthesis could be called "infinite" in

---

2. Hegel is here introducing a fundamental concept of Kant's ethics.
3. This sounds like the quest for the god beyond god of some mystics.

a third sense: a self-constituting process that both generates finite moments and at the same time goes beyond them, incorporating them into a larger synthesis. If now we do not simply hold those two moments in a dynamic synthesis but conceive that synthesis as a unified function, we have reached a new immediate concept: the thought of a self-contained being, or a being on its own account. For this Hegel uses another German term *Fürsichsein* which, literally translated, is "being-for-itself"; a comparable English expression might be "being-of-itself."

Being-for-self

In the next chapter, Hegel moves from talking about quality to setting the stage for a discussion of quantity. It all begins from thinking about what "being-of-itself" involves.

In one sense it is like pure being; but more is involved, for it is explicitly self-contained. That is to say it has incorporated any determinations into itself. It organizes its being from its own unified perspective—this Hegel calls "being-for-one." This new description says nothing more than what was already involved in "being-of-itself," but makes it more explicit. Indeed, it affirms the self-contained being as a unit—as "one."[4]

When we think of a unit as one we exclude all alteration from it. There is nothing in it that could produce otherness. But now we have come upon a new sense of "nothing." Early on, "nothing" simply captured the indeterminacy of "pure being." Now, however, it is the explicit exclusion of any determination, best described as the "void." Once we identify this new concept, we can distinguish it from the "one" on its own, thus setting the "one" within a surrounding void.

Here Hegel makes a typical dialectical move. The "one" is both "one" and the "void" in having no distinct internal determination. That is to say, in being self-contained it excludes, indeed repels, otherness. But this suggests that something is excluded. That something will itself have to be self-contained, since it is explicitly defined as not incorporated into the original "one" in any way. Whereas these other "ones" emerge from reflection on our original concept, they nonetheless have to be fixed as themselves self-contained, repelling otherness. So we now have a number of ones which populate the "void."[5]

"Repulsion" involves excluding other "ones." Although this concept emerged as a way of ensuring that the "one" remain self-contained, it turns out that it is an essential feature of the "one." Only through repulsion can it

---

4. Interesting is the fact that Hegel identifies this way of being self-contained through being incorporated into a single perspective, as being the framework for idealism. For a self-contained being all determinations are simply ideal. This is in contrast to the *reality* of a being's "quality," which was expanded into the concepts of "determination," "constitution," "limit" and "finitude."

5. Hegel has here shown the implicit reasoning that underlies the atomism of Leucippus and Democritus. The same reflections led to Leibniz's monadology.

maintain itself as "one." But this means that it requires the many other "ones" to establish its own distinctive significance. They are not simply repelled as others, they are required as co-ordinates. This contrary pressure is called "attraction."

When we see how the many "ones" are mutually attracted to each other, we think of all of them within the same perspective. In other words, we now have *one* "one" that combines all the previous many "ones." From this overall perspective, the many become ideal components of a more encompassing self-contained being.

Yet this larger one cannot collapse the many into a simple unity. For "attraction" requires that there be a many to be attracted, and this means that it presupposes "repulsion." At the same time, "repulsion," which started out as required simply because of the exclusivity of the "one" shows that it presupposes "attraction." For if there were not already some pressure to collapse the many into a one, there would be no need for repulsion. So "attraction" and "repulsion" balance each other in an equilibrium.[6]

At this point Hegel reflects on the total picture that has developed. We have many "ones" each of which is simply a self-contained unit. Any qualities have been simply absorbed into their self-contained independence. On the one hand, these are distinct each from the other through the dynamic of "repulsion." On the other hand they are all part of a single totality through the integrating drive of "attraction." We have a magnitude or multiplicity which is both (via "repulsion") discrete and (through "attraction") continuous. But that satisfies the definition of the term "quantity." Starting from the concept of "being-of-itself" he has arrived at quantity or magnitude.

Early on in the third chapter of the *Logic* on *Fürsichsein*, Hegel has a comment about the various stages that the discussion will follow, suggesting that it will parallel the earlier discussions of "pure being" and *Dasein* or "determinate being." It may be helpful to cite that passage, and then show the parallels with the passages already discussed:

Attention may be drawn in advance not only to the difficulty involved in the following exposition of the *development* of the one as well as to its cause. The *moments* which constitute the *concept* of the "one" as "being-for-itself" fall apart in that development. They are: (1) negation in general, (2) *two* negations, (3) two that are therefore *the same*, (4) which are quite opposed; (5) self-relation, identity as such, (6) a relation that is *negative* and yet *oriented towards itself.*[7]

---

6. In this section, Hegel is showing the conceptual foundation for the position Kant takes in his *Metaphysical Foundations of Natural Science*.

7. *SL* 163; *GW* 21: 151. This passage is an addition made in 1831 to the second edition; as in other cases, the revision highlights Hegel's methodological concerns. A careful reader will find the same six stages in sub-components of the argument—on the relation between "being for another" and "being in itself," for example, or how "being-for-self" and "being-for-one" interconnect.

1. Negation in general: being to nothing; something to other; finite to infinite; one to the void.
2. Two negations: by adding nothing to being; other as something with an other; infinite as finite; the void as a "one."
3. Two that are therefore the same: being = nothing; something = other; finite = infinite; void = one.
4. Which are quite opposed: being is NOT nothing; something is NOT other; finite is NOT infinite; one REPELS the many.
5. Self-relation, identity as such: becoming; determination; infinite regress; attraction.
6. A relation that is negative and yet directed toward itself: coming-to-be and passing-away; limit; genuine infinite that incorporates the finite and the beyond; attraction and repulsion as two sides of a single complex relationship which could be called magnitude.

Here, then, we have an expanded version of our original analysis. The first two moves are reciprocal *dialectical* shifts which lead to the apparent contradiction of two concepts being identical yet radically opposed. That reflective synthesis becomes the basis on which *speculative* reason can identify the basic relation as well as its complex of determinate internal moments. *Understanding* is then able to crystallize this dynamic into a new starting point, which can be isolated on its own. And it has been able to take the whole rational process and distinguish within it six determinate stages. In this passage, then, we have confirmation of our earlier discussion of Hegel's method in the *Science of Logic*.

Chapter 7

Quantity

Hegel has divided his treatise into three books: on Being, Essence and Concept. The first major section of the first book has been devoted to what Hegel calls quality. By this he is referring to whatever distinguishes something from something else—the limit beyond which any alteration would change one kind of being into another. By contrast quantity considers many units considered to be from the same order or kind; they are both discrete (as many) and continuous (as coming from the same sort of thing). Qualitatively these units are indifferent to each other; "quantity" captures this indifference.

For us, "quantity" contains a number of constituent meanings. My *Random House Dictionary of the English Language* lists among its entries the following:

1. a particular, indefinite, or considerable amount of anything .... 2. the amount or measure .... 3. considerable or great amount .... 4. *Math.* a. the property of magnitude involving comparability with other magnitudes. b. something having magnitude, or size, extent, amount or the like. c. magnitude, size, volume, area, or length. ... 7. that amount, degree, etc., in terms of which another is greater or lesser.[1]

To make his logic fully systematic Hegel does not start out with that full panoply of sense. Eventually all aspects will be covered; but they emerge only gradually along a path that follows methodological twists and turns similar to those already encountered.

To be sure, Hegel's title for the whole section is not "Quantity" but "Magnitude." And he adopts "Quantity" only for the first chapter, to be followed by "Quantum" (or a specific quantity) and then "Ratio." Nonetheless when he comes to the end of the section he points out that, whereas thinking about quality leads to the thought of quantity, it is the thought of quantity (not magnitude) that leads back to quality. We need to see how he can bring that about.

---

1. *The Random House Dictionary of the English Language*, ed. J. Stein and L. Urdang, (New York: Random House, 1973) 1175. Omitted are the examples of usage and particular senses from music, logic, phonetics and law.

Before doing so, however, we need to recall that Hegel taught mathematics in both the University of Jena and the Nürnberg secondary school. As he proceeded through this discussion he cannot help commenting, not only on the prevailing philosophies of mathematics, but also on the theoretical underpinnings of a number of standard mathematical operations, calculus in particular. These lengthy remarks make this section by far the longest in the whole *Science of Logic*. But for our purposes we shall leave them aside, and concentrate on the main text; it is there that we will capture the essential principles of his logical analysis.

Quantity

We have reached the thought of "magnitude" by way of atomism's conceptual logic: starting from self-contained units, we have moved on to a many that, to retain their multiplicity, repel each other; yet they are attracted to each other since they are qualitatively indistinct—each unit is simply self-contained and on its own account. Quality has become redundant, and we are left with the continuity inherent in attraction and the discreteness involved in repulsion. "Quantity" unites these two components, and that unity introduces the sense of "magnitude" as both continuous and discrete. We have a many making up one unity. It does so by excluding other multiples. It is one definite quantum, indifferent in one sense to its limit, yet nonetheless defined by it. This quantum we call "number." With this move Hegel introduces the thought of "a particular amount" that was part of the *Random House* definition.

Quantum

A number is self-contained, it includes a definite set of units and, distinct from other numbers, it is exclusive. It is, then, the combination of its singularity or unity, and its amount—the many it incorporates. Curiously enough, no one of the multitude is the number's determining limit; for, were we to take some particular hundred, at one time or another any one of the set would, if it went missing, reduce the number to ninety-nine.

Hegel then explores the close relationship between "unity" and "amount" that makes up the concept of "number." "Amount" picks up the "discrete" aspect of pure quantity. But since the limit that defines a specific number now has a role to play we have moved on to a distinct thought: of an extensive magnitude.[2] Were we to concentrate instead on the "unity" of the number and downplay the "amount," the number becomes an intensive magnitude, capturing a specific degree of intensity.[3]

---

2. Consider *Random House*'s "something having magnitude or size, extent, amount or the like."
3. Again: "that amount, degree, etc., in terms of which another is greater or lesser."

When we look more closely we find that these two contrary concepts shift into each other. For an extensive magnitude must presuppose that all the units are continuous—of the same kind; and an intensive magnitude requires that each degree become an independent unit, making up a determinate amount. "Quantum" or determinate quantity is indifferent to which way it is being read. Its focus is on the way it excludes and is external to other quanta (the plural of this Latin term).[4]

These other quanta are no different in kind from the original one. Yet any quantum is susceptible to change. Were one unit to disappear from, or be added to, the amount, it would become a different number. The continuity that binds one quantum with its neighbours leads to the recognition that numbers are in principle variable.

At this point Hegel reintroduces a discussion of infinity.[5] Earlier he talked about qualitative infinity: where something goes *beyond* the limits of its quality and, no longer determined by it, becomes something else. Quantum, too, has a limit. But when thought moves *beyond* that limit we remain in the same, continuous, qualitative sphere. So we have another quantum which is also in principle variable, and allows a further move beyond. The pattern can repeat itself into an infinity which has no limit. This Hegel calls the "bad quantitative infinity."

The series of determinate quantities can be extended into the infinitely large, or the infinitely small. But it is important to notice important features. In the first place, all that we mean by infinity is that we can always go beyond any determinate number to the next; the transition is always repeatable. In the second place, when we talk about infinity as such we are talking about no number at all, since it is unlimited. If we talk about "the infinite" we are referring to something that is qualitatively distinct from the original quanta. By cancelling the limitation inherent in the determinate quantum, the infinite "negates its negation," as Hegel likes to say. But this move also introduces a sense of quality into our discussion of quantity. For we are now distinguishing the determinate "quanta" from "the infinite" in qualitative, not quantitative terms.

For Hegel this has an interesting consequence. For when we unpack the sense of "quantum" we find that it contains: first, the variability of a limited quantity into the next greater or next smaller quantum; second, the repetition of this kind of shift without limit; and so, third, the inclusion of the qualitatively different sense of "the infinite"—what was to be completely external to quantity has now been incorporated into its sense. Once we have identified these different characteristics, and bring them together into

---

4. Curiously, in the German text, Hegel frequently conjugates this noun according to Latin paradigms (Quantorum, Quantis, etc.) but then slips into inflecting it using German conventions (des Quantums).

5. From the *Random House Dictionary*: "indefinite or considerable amount."

a single perspective, we can integrate the whole cluster of meanings into a single new concept—one in which quanta that are external to each other are yet necessarily related. This is the concept of "quantitative ratio."[6]

Quantitative Ratio

In a ratio we have two quanta related to each other to form a single quantum. In the eighteenth and early nineteenth century, that single quantum was called the ratio's "exponent."[7] In a direct ratio, one of the two components will vary whenever the other changes in such a way that the exponent always remains the same: 6/3, 12/6 and 410/205 all have the same exponent (2/1). In its formulation, one of the components is defined as the "unit" or "unity," the other becomes the "amount." It turns out, however, that the exponent is nothing other that the "amount" of the most basic version of the ratio (in our example, 2), even though it was supposed to capture the relationship between the two components. If we want to have a ratio where the exponent (which defines the relationship) is clearly distinct from the components, we need to have one where it has a distinct role with reference to the other two. This happens in an inverted ratio.

An inverted ratio occurs where an increase in one of the components produces a decrease in the other. Here the exponent, as the product of the two components *(xy=k)*, remains a fixed constant while the direct ratio between the two components may vary considerably.

In this kind of ratio, the exponent plays a different role. As one of the components is reduced towards zero, the other approximates ever more closely the amount of the fixed constant. Yet it can never reach that goal; for then there would be no ratio at all—the first component would disappear altogether. The exponent thus becomes both a limit to the range of the variables, and at the same time a beyond, since it can never in fact be reached by them. Unlike the way it was in the earlier qualitative discussion of infinity, the limit here *is* the beyond. Yet, as a determinate quantum, the exponent is not absent, but present.[8] The infinite is something affirmative, not a negative other.

When Hegel looks back at what is involved in inverted ratio, however, he notices that the exponent is fixed, and present as an infinite limit. Each of the components of the ratio can at one time or another approximate the limit, yet they are defined relative to each other by the fact that, when multiplied

---

6. From our *Dictionary*: "the property of magnitude involving comparability with other magnitudes." Note that Hegel has here brought together conceptual components of mathematical calculus, such as the infinitessimal and ratios. Indeed he ventures into lengthy remarks to discuss its philosophical underpinnings.

7. In contemporary mathematics, "exponent" is used to refer to the superscript number which indicates how many times a quantum is multiplied by itself: 2^3, 10^{27}, and so on.

8. Hegel is able to play on a nice relationship in the German: "the beyond" is *das Jenseits*; the "present" is on this side, that is *das Diesseits*.

together, their product is the same as the exponent. What we have is a ratio, or relation, between two moments within the same quantum. So the exponent is not simply external to the components. Were we to develop a ratio where the same number determines both of its components, then we would have a relation or ratio of powers: $x:x^3$.

With this move, the concept "quantum" has become fully self-contained. It started out as composed of the two aspects of "number": "unity" and "amount." In the inverted ratio the "amount" is still determined not by the other term in the ratio but from outside by the fixed exponent, an independent "third." But when we have a ratio of powers the "unity" in principle defines the "amount" and the "amount" is set over against its own "unity." The "exponent" of this ratio is no longer an immediate quantum, but is rather qualitative—a simple requirement that the quantum be related directly to itself. But, interestingly enough, "pure self-relation" is the way the original concept that started the whole logical development is defined; for "pure being" is simple self-equivalence. We have come full circle.

On the surface, a ratio of powers seems to be subject to a purely arbitrary variation. We can change the key quantum in whatever way we want, and the resulting ratio will vary accordingly. But what defines this ratio is that the quantum be related solely to itself.

Earlier we saw that qualitative difference emerged in our discussion of quantum when we came to the concept of the "quantitative infinite." That qualitative feature became more precise with the exponent of an inverse ratio, which serves as a limit which the components can approximate asymptotically (as a mathematician would say). But now quality defines the character of the ratio itself.

The end result of the whole analysis of quantity or magnitude, then, is a return to the concept of quality, with which we began the logic. At the same time, we have already discovered that, when quality is analysed we end up with one and many, attraction and repulsion, and then continuity and discreteness—in other words quantity. We have here what Hegel calls a double transition: From quality we pass over to quantity; from quantity we pass over to quality. The two are reciprocally related. And as such they make up a synthetic totality.

In the second edition of this part of the *Logic* Hegel adds a comment: "For the totality to be *posited*, there needs to be the *double* transition, not only the passing over of the one determination into its other, but also the passing over of this other, its return, into the first.... This remark concerning the necessity of the *double* transition is of great importance for the whole of the scientific method."[9] We have seen this move before. It is here, however, where Hegel specifically mentions how important it is.

9. *SL* 323; *GW* 21: 320. The stresses are found in the original. Compare this comment with §241 in the 1827 and 1830 editions of *EL*.

A synthetic totality can be collapsed into a conceptual unity. What we are thinking of is a union of quantity and quality—we give quality a number. This process is called "measuring." So the next section of the *Logic* turns to the concept of "measure."

It is worth pausing, however, and recalling the *Random House Dictionary* definition of quantity with which we began. It included elements like "particular or indefinite amount," "magnitude involving comparability with other magnitudes," "that amount, degree, etc., in terms of which another is greater or lesser." What Hegel has done is to take these terms and several others and incorporate them into a narrative, where the need for each concept is required by reflection on the ones that preceded: We have moved through "continuous and discrete magnitude" to "quantum," "number," "amount" and "unity," and on to "extensive and intensive magnitude," "degree," the indefiniteness of "quantitative infinity," "ratios, both direct and inverse," and "powers." On the way we have covered the conceptual foundations of calculus as well as the more basic forms of arithmetic, geometry and algebra. Hegel's achievement lies not in the fact that he discusses these various concepts. Rather it lies in his being able to connect them in a systematic way, so that the thought of one requires and leads on to the thought of something more sophisticated. They are all part of a single attempt by thought to think through its own functioning. And, in a surprising way, he shows that it is thought itself which brings together the concepts of "quality" and "quantity" into the relationship we call "measuring." What is genuinely novel in his study is not the particular concepts discussed and their definitions. Most of the time they correspond quite closely with those adopted by the mathematicians. Hegel's originality lies in finding the conceptual connections which integrate all those various terms into a single, consecutive story.

Chapter 8

Measure

We have reached the concept of measure because we found that quantity and quality are linked together conceptually. Once we thoroughly analyze quality, we end up talking about continuity and discreteness—the features of magnitude. And when we examine quantity in its turn, we come to ratios, which define a certain qualitative limit to a quantity. The act of combining a quantity with a quality we call measuring. After all, when we measure we are trying to find the quantity that exactly matches a particular quality.[1]

Hegel thus arrives at the concept of measure. But he admits that its analysis provides one of the most difficult parts of his *Logic*. So it is not surprising that he constantly draws on material from the natural sciences to illustrate the particular kinds of measuring involved. While he thought the section was important enough to receive a careful revision in 1831, he nonetheless covered it very schematically in the outline he published for use in his lectures. We shall therefore move rather carefully through this section.

Specific Quantity

From the ancient Greeks we learn that everything has a measure—which suggests that its distinctive quality can be identified if we can find its appropriate quantity. But that insight does not take us very far. For it simply says that to every quality a certain definite quantum can be ascribed. When we try to do so, however, the result is not satisfactory. In the first place, the quantity we attribute to any quality is based on an arbitrary unit of measurement. We could use inches or we could use centimetres, and the result would be quite different.[2] So there is no one number that uniquely identifies what we want to

---

1. Recall that the *Random House Dictionary* article on "quantity" included the definition: "the amount or measure."
2. Early measurements reflected particular circumstances: the length of a thumb or an arm, for example. Each community would have its own barrel measure.

measure. In the second place, the qualities themselves can vary in quantity; a red can be more or less intense. At some point, indeed, a change in quantity can produce a change in quality (as when we leave a person with hair on his head when we remove only one or two strands, but if we continue the process he will at some point become bald). Yet in most cases the measurement can vary without affecting the quality.

This vague, initial sense of measuring, then, has its problems. What we intended to get at when we thought of everything as measured is that there is one specific measure for each quality. But this has not been achieved. So we must consider what we can do to improve the rigour of our measuring.

The most obvious way of doing this is by setting some standard or rule which defines the fundamental units—the metre in Paris or the length of a day. We establish a basic quantitative unit and then measure how many such units any particular qualitative thing has. But again such universal standards are set by an arbitrary decision. Even when we say that the unit is a fraction of the circumference of the earth, or of the length of a day, which fraction we choose is a matter of indifference. The quality being measured couldn't care less which standard has been adopted. The desired unity of quantity and quality has not been achieved.

Instead of taking an arbitrary unit for measuring, however, we could use one quality to measure another. Instead of matching a single number to a single characteristic we will identify the ratio these qualities have to each other. The result will be constant—in Hegel's language, the ratio will have a particular exponent. At times the ratio can be direct (as when speed is measured as distance over time) or it can be a ratio of powers (as when acceleration is measured as distance divided by the square of the time). But even here we have not escaped variability. For how do we define the initial unit of the measuring quality (time, for example) and how many units of the measured quality (space) are to be counted within that period of time? Measuring miles-per-hour is not the same as measuring kilometres-per-hour; and miles-per-gallon provides a quite different ratio from litres-per-hundred-kilometres. Once again we have a kind of measuring that does not really isolate what is central to the qualities being measured.

The reason for this variability lies in the fact that the two sides of the ratio are independent of each other; the two distinctive qualities are related to each other simply to satisfy the requirements we have in mind when measuring. Time has a "life of its own" quite apart from its role in measuring velocity or acceleration; how we measure the quantity of any fuel is indifferent to how much of it is used by any particular car in highway driving. The two kinds of independent values are brought together in the ratio, not because of anything inherent to the quality being measured, but because we have introduced an alien expectation from outside.

The situation changes, however, once we take two qualitative character-istics that belong to the same thing. Then we are not bringing the mea-sured and the measuring sides together in an arbitrary way; they are already united in reality, and our task is to distinguish them and identify the ratios that hold between them. When we do this, it will not matter what particular units we use, since the ratio will always remain the same. It will be something self-contained, and can be considered on its own.

In his discussion of determinate being and its qualities, Hegel suggests that we use the term "real" to identify a qualified being. At this point in our discussion of measure, we are now thinking of something with several qualities or determinations, and using one of them to measure the other. So we can say that we are measuring the "reality" of the thing. This is why Hegel calls the next stage "real measuring."

Real Measure

The kind of measuring now being considered seeks to specify the inherent quality of something by relating its specific quantity to another, more superficial, quality that can be found in other things as well. Thus when we measure the specific gravity of gold we construct a ratio between its weight and its volume. Other things, like silver or wood, will have a quite different weight for the same volume. This sort of measuring works particularly well when we compare the ratio found in one real thing with that found in another one.

Such comparisons vary, however, depending on which particular things we decide to compare. Since no single measurement results, the measuring remains arbitrary. If we can find a way of comparing that is inherent to the things being measured, we will have a more satisfactory specification. This in fact happens when the two things (such as an acid and an alkali) are combined into a single thing, and one then measures the (neutral) result. Once this is done we can specify the original quality, not simply in terms of its basic ratio (of specific gravity, in our example) but how that ratio relates to the corresponding ratio in the other thing as well as in the compound. We now have a more complex ratio of ratios.

Of course there is not just one other thing with which our original entity (let us say sulphuric acid) can be combined. There are a number of other candidates, each of which (being an alkali) will produce a different calcu-lation when the primary ratio is combined with the ratio of each respective compound. We can now be more precise in specifying the distinctive quality of the original thing by listing the variety of complex ratios that result.

We already know that any measurement can specify only by drawing a distinction between the quality we are interested in measuring and other similar qualities. If this series of ratios (developed from sulphuric acid) is to be at all meaningful, it needs to be compared with other series. And this can work only if we consider what happens when other kinds of things (or acids) are combined with the same series of alternative entities (the alkalis) that the first thing was. These new things will have to differ from the initial acid in a distinctive way; that is, they will be such that it *does not* enter into compounds with them. We have, then, two sets of things, where each individual item can combine with any of the objects in the other set, but not with those on its own side. And we can measure each one against its partners by developing the series of ratios each of them has when combined with the whole set of opposites, one after another. We can now compare how the different series of exponents compare with regard to the quantitative intervals that hold between the various members of each of these series. The more we extend our comparisons, the more exact our measurements will be.

It is all getting very complicated, however. For we have ratios of ratios which are then compared at a third level. But when we think back over all this complexity we realize that it is supposed to be the initial quality which ultimately determines how all the more complex constructions develop. For its measured quantity serves as the numerator for the first ratio, and that ratio then becomes the denominator for the second series of ratios, and the intervals in that second series provide a basis of comparison with alternate series. In addition, we realize that each thing or kind of thing can become the basis for a similar complex development.

Hidden in all of this entangled web is the fact that there are some things that enter into compounds with the thing we are trying to measure, and other things which do not. There is something we might call an affinity that draws certain things together. In other words, when we review the series of compounds that result from a thing, we find that it prefers some of these compounds to others. At times it abandons its combination with one to take up an association with another. It is this "elective affinity" that would seem to measure more precisely the quality we want to specify. (This chemical process takes place when two salts, both resulting from the union of an acid with an alkali, exchange radicals once they are placed in the same solution.)[3]

By this time the examples Hegel uses have moved beyond specific gravity to chemical affinity and to harmonic progressions. The experience of chemistry, however, suggests that, even here, there are complications. For we have been talking about bringing two things together into a compound, but we have not talked about their proportions within this compound. Those are simple amounts, and like any number can easily be altered.

3. "For example, when *caustic terra ponderosa* ($Ba(OH)_2$) was added to *vitriolated tartar* (K_2SO_4), *ponderous spar* ($BaSO_4$) was formed, leaving a liquor that contained *caustic vegetable alkali* (KOH)." A.J. Ihde, *The Development of Modern Chemistry* (New York: Dover, 1984) 94. Ihde is referring to discoveries made by Torbern Bergmann in Sweden during the late eighteenth century.

What we find is that, as we gradually change the proportions of the two substances, some qualities of the compound can change quite radically. When preparing his lectures for the Philosophy of Nature in 1803–04, Hegel refers to what happens when mercury is combined with oxygen: "The transition of the oxidation of mercury does not move from the first stage where it is green (black), into becoming progressively brighter, but it passes over into another colour, red, and becomes a semi-glazed oxide; grey lead oxide equally does not pass into merely something brighter, but into something yellow, then into bright red (where it is glazed) and then into a completely glazed, honey-yellow oxide."[4]

We have here an interesting result. On the one hand we have a gradual change of quantity, one that follows the continuity characteristic of mathematical infinity. On the other hand we have a shift of one quality into another—the move to another, finite beyond—which fits the analysis of qualitative infinity. We have a new kind of infinite that moves from gradual change to qualitative transformation and back again. But since there is nothing in the first quality that can tell us exactly what the new quality will be like, we have run up against a qualitative change that is measureless.

But something else has happened as well. For the changing qualities have emerged from simply a gradual alteration in the quantities of the component substances. The underlying reality has not significantly altered in terms of what makes it up. There has only been a slight adjustment in the ratio. So we are led to introduce a distinction between the surface qualities and the reality—the thing itself—that underlies them. It is this distinction that prevents "real measuring" capturing what is specific about any particular quality.[5]

The Becoming of Essence

Hegel finally turns to this distinction between surface and underlying reality. Reality, as it is now being defined in the *Logic*, is absolutely indifferent to what happens superficially. Indifference has certainly emerged earlier in the analysis. Pure being is simply equal to itself and so indifferent to whatever else may come along. Quantity is indifferent to any quality. But now we have indifference pure and simple: its lack of differentiation an explicit contrast to the changing variety on the surface. As radically distinct from any differentiation, it can be called absolute indifference.[6]

---

4. *GW6*: 166.
5. For a more detailed exposition of this chapter, see my *Real Process* (Toronto: University of Toronto Press, 1996) 30–52.
6. Indeed Hegel adopts the Latin term "*Indifferenz*" rather than his more commonly used German term, "*Gleichgültigkeit*," to capture the peculiar sense involved. This term could have, in addition to the sense of "being indifferent," the sense of "being undifferentiated."

Yet this indifference has a determinate being. The surface is character-ized by determinate quantities and qualities whose proportions vary. As one quantity increased, the other decreases. If one quality becomes domi-nant, the other recedes. A kind of inverse ratio governs the way superficial alteration happens.

All of this surface activity has no connection with the underlying indif-ference; it remains unaltered and unaffected. Nonetheless this surface is the form that this indifferent substratum takes. Whatever quality emerges, that quality is the complete concrete expression of the reality underneath. This leads to all kinds of contradictory results.

For, when we talk of a quality on its own being dominant, then it should completely overwhelm the recessive quality and reduce it to impotence. But in this situation the underlying indifference sets a limit, and indeed prevents the weaker quality from disappearing. Rather, the weaker con-verts into being dominant and forces the other to retreat. Only through this constant change can the diversity of the surface remain distinct from the total indifference of the substrate. Yet that substrate cannot be totally indif-ferent if it limits the range of the surface activity. In other words, the substrate is not completely unconnected to the surface, for it does not allow the sur-face qualities to simply follow their own logic. Absolute indifference turns out to be an incoherent concept.

Hegel's description appears strange when we first encounter it. Yet he has several conceptual structures in mind. On the one hand, his colleague, Schelling, had at times said that the Absolute was absolute indifference, underlying both the idealism of conceptual construction and the rhythms of natural processes. "Dealing with something from the perspective of the Absolute," Hegel caustically observes in the Preface to the *Phenome-nology*, "consists merely in declaring that, although one has been speaking of it just now as something definite, yet in the Absolute, the A=A, there is nothing of the kind, for there all is one. To pit this single insight, that in the Absolute everything is the same, against the full body of articulated cogni-tion, which at least seeks and demands such fulfillment, to palm off its Absolute as the night in which, as the saying goes, all cows are black—this is cognition naïvely reduced to vacuity."[7]

But Hegel also applies it to a situation more closely connected with measuring. Astronomy had attempted to explain the elliptical orbits of the planets by saying that their movement resulted from the interplay of two forces, one centrifugal and the other centripetal—one pulling towards the centre, the other pulling away from the centre. The centripetal force becomes dominant, pulling the planet further away from the sun, until it reaches the limit of the curve (its aphelion) at which time the centrifugal

---

7. *Hegel's Phenomenology of Spirit*, tr. A.V. Miller (Oxford: Clarendon, 1977) 9; *GW* 9: 17.

force starts to pull it back again, becoming more dominant in turn as the planet swings back closer to the sun (its perihelion). Then the centripetal force re-emerges to become dominant once again. Such a theory, Hegel says, tells us very little about the nature of the elliptical orbit, since it does not tell us why the weaker force should suddenly become dominant again. Indeed, at every point both the centrifugal and the centripetal forces need to be in play to maintain the planet in its orbit, and keep it from flying— either off to outer space or into the cauldron of the sun.

The contradictions that emerge from this set of concepts mark the culmination of what Hegel has called the Doctrine of Being. He has been exploring the simple transitions of thought that lead from concept to concept as their specific meanings become explicit. Underlying all of this is the conviction that concepts, once identified, are indifferent to each other. It is external thought that moves us on from one to the next. But we have come to the thought of something—the absolutely indifferent—which, it turns out, must itself influence the way its related concepts function. These surface concepts, in turn, define the nature of this underlying reality. There is a kind of mutual implication built into the meaning of each side.

In this context we no longer have a simple transition from one thought to another. Rather a concept posits or sets up its counterpart; and the latter presupposes the former.[8] Each reflects the other. And the underlying reality is no longer an indifferent substrate but something essential. So we have moved beyond the Doctrine of Being to the Doctrine of Essence, where we shall not only explore how this pattern of mutual reflection works, but also what we mean when we talk about essences that explain why things are the way they are.

---

8. In German "posit" and "presuppose" have the same root: *Setzen* and *Voraussetzen*.

PART III

The Doctrine of Essence

Chapter 9

The Essence of Self-Reflection

Show

As we might expect, the logic that explores the meaning of "essence" turns out to be more complicated than what has gone on before. There, thought simply moves over from one thought to its complement or contrary. An essence, however, is to be distinguished from what is immediately present. At first it might appear as if that immediate being and the essence are two independent terms. But once we look more closely we see that the immediate qualities and quantities have shown themselves to be transient and inessential, requiring the move to something more substantial underlying it.

Hegel turns first to this immediate show. It is rather like the Hindu concept of *maya*, where the world of experience is thought of as a veil, hiding yet suggesting what is ultimate and essential. So we have a reciprocal relationship between the essence and this show. The essence (like the absolute indifference of the previous chapter) is understood to be other than the surface being; yet this being, as *maya*, is not to be considered in its own right, but rather as both veiling and (in a sense) revealing what is genuinely important. We could say, then, that the essence is nothing other than our understanding of the immediate qualities confronting us as *maya*.

Here we have been introduced to a distinctive pattern of thought. Earlier we simply moved on from being to nothing, and then moved back again. But now we remain with essence as we distinguish it from *maya*, and we remain with the *maya* as it both shows and veils the essence. Each reflects, and is reflected in, the other.

We have already had reason to use reflection.[1] Whenever thought makes an immediate transition to a new concept, reflection steps in

---

1. In Hegel's German, the word used for show or *maya* is *Schein*, a cognate of the English "shine," and reflections shine so the logical move to reflection is prefigured in a word play of ordinary language.

to look back over what has gone on and identify its characteristics. But that strategy is introduced from outside of the original concepts being thought. It is we, the thinkers, who recall what has happened and bring it to the fore. Now, however, each concept points to, and responds to, its counterpart. "Show" reflects the essence, and "essence" reflects the show. In other words, the mode of thinking we call reflection is not simply an approach we introduce from outside; it is also found within the very concepts being thought. The next move in Hegel's logical progress is to explore what is involved in reflection.

Reflection takes the immediate starting point to be something inessential; its role is to dissolve that surface show so that thought can reach what it veils, which is the essence. The whole process is marked by negatives: the starting point is an inessential nonentity; reflection dissolves itself; and the result is other than the original given. Each of its components is defined by what it is not. What holds these three negative moments together is the presupposition that there is a reality, lying beneath the surface, which is posited as genuinely immediate in contrast to what is presented directly in the reflective process. So, to grasp what is really unmediated, reflection not only dissolves the "immediate" surface show, but also cancels the effects of its own mediating activity. It thinks of itself as standing outside of the material it is thinking about.

The fact that reflection, to be effective, must cancel the mediating effects of its own activity has an impact on the way it functions. For the changes introduced by its activity cannot be allowed to mediate or influence the characteristics of the essence that is to emerge from the process of reflecting. That essence has been presupposed as genuinely immediate. In other words, the task of reflection is to remove from the surface being that has initiated its activity those inessentials which are in fact not genuinely immediate. To do this successfully it must presuppose some determination that essentially characterizes the real immediate, and which can nonetheless be discerned as both shown and veiled in the surface *maya*. So reflection is not only external to the material it is thinking about; it relies as well on reflective determinations that both constitutes the essential to be discerned and regulates its own operations.

The determinations that both define the essence and constrain the activity of thinking are unmediated, and so they are to be distinguished from the mediating activity of reflection. They persist and are presupposed by thought. Indeed, precisely because they are not to be the function of any synthesizing intellectual activity, there may be any number of such determinations, compatible, yet unrelated to each other.

The result is a paradox. For reflection has now two conflicting functions. On the one hand, it actively reflects on the surface *maya* in the course of deriving the underlying essence. On the other hand, in this process it uses fixed and persistent determinations that are unaffected by the dynamic of thought, but are nonetheless its critical component. Each function requires (or is reflected in) the other. For reflection as such cannot discern the essence unless it uses the determinations; and the determinations can only be effective if they become norms regulating the reflective activity.

At this point, rather than reaching a reciprocal cycle that can be united into a single new concept (as happened in the earlier part of the *Logic*), thought has come up with a fundamental paradox: two features which are explicit opposites, both of which are yet constitutive of a single intellectual operation. The way forward involves looking at the determinations of reflection—at the laws which determine how thought should function—to see what is explicitly involved.

Before moving on to review what Hegel has to say about these laws of thought, let us review what he has been doing so far in this initial discussion of essence. He has been investigating what Kant would call the categories that underlie a common, and fundamental, type of thinking. Whenever we look for an explanation we are showing that we are not satisfied with the surface show of things, but are interested in determining what is their essential ground. Such is the procedure, not only of all religion, but also of all natural science and all social theory. Any reflection of this sort follows the pattern Hegel outlines: We presume that the given is not the real picture—indeed that it may be fundamentally misleading. We presume that thinking about this puzzle will not affect or influence the real explanations that are to be the results of the endeavour. And we hope for success because we accept as given some fundamental principles that not only govern all thought, but are constitutive of what is essentially the case.

There is, after all, far more to thinking than simply uniting subject and predicate. Thinking also involves reflecting: searching for explanations, looking for underlying principles, questing for unchanging truth. While it is true that the modern world has stopped talking about essences in any ontological sense, it nonetheless continues to look for what is really going on underneath the surface of natural and social phenomena. And this quest presupposes what Hegel calls the categories of essence, show (or *maya*) and reflection.

But there is something else to notice. Earlier in Chapter 5, we suggested that the simple transitions of thought—from being to nothing, from something to other, from finite to infinite—were parallel to the work of what Hegel calls dialectical reason. Speculative reason in contrast brings together into a synthesis the opposing features that have emerged through dialectic. It looks for the affirmative contained in their mutual dissolution—their transition into each other.[2] Although we have not yet followed its

---

2. Cf. *EL* §82. Notice that speculation comes from the Latin *speculum*, which means "mirror." Is this another Hegelian pun?

logic through to the end, reflection has parallels with this description. It takes up opposition—between essence and show, or between persisting determinations and its own dissolving activity—and holds them together in a synthesis, if not yet a unity. It looks for the affirmative essence that is contained in the dissolution and transience of mere surface show. That parallel between reflection and speculative reason will only become more explicit as we investigate what Hegel calls the determinations of reflection.

Determinations of Reflection

Since reflection presupposes that the essence to be discerned remains consistent despite surface variations, the most basic determination it relies on is the law of identity. What is essential are the patterns or characteristics that remain the same. Yet identity only makes sense when contrasted with difference. Similarly pure difference requires reference to some kind of identity. So thought must consider how to bring identity and difference together in a synthesis in a way that advances the aims of reflection.

The way things are identified may have nothing at all to do with the way they are differentiated. We then have a diversity, in which one can discern through comparison how some things are alike and others are unlike. When, as the next step, we turn to this relationship between likeness and unlikeness (or equality and inequality) we find an opposition, for like and unlike are the positive and negative sides of a single reflective act of comparison. Sometimes when we distinguish opposites as positive and negative it is a matter of indifference which we call the positive and which the negative as long as they are opposed to each other in a single perspective (a perspective which Hegel calls the "positive-and-negative"). But if we are going to get at what makes some things essentially positive and others essentially negative we find that we must go further. For the positive is positive because it excludes (negatively) the negative; and the negative positively constitutes itself when it excludes its positive opposite. So each of them involve both the positive and the negative at the same time.

The reflection that draws these inferences about the genuinely positive and negative is affected by a similar paradox. For as a single act it must exclude from itself these contradictory entities, yet positively affirm them as contradictory. So the result is no longer simply an opposition, but a contradiction, in which what is denied is affirmed, and what is affirmed is denied. Such a kind of reflection in effect destroys that upon which it stands, and so must "fall to the ground." With this metaphor Hegel suggests that when contradictions emerge they cannot be maintained; rather reflection must investigate their underlying ground or reason. So the critical law of thought is the principle of sufficient reason, in which reflection determines the ground of explicit paradoxes.

Hegel has, then, outlined the categorical basis for the traditional laws of thought and how they can be derived one from another. The law of identity leads into the principle of diversity, contained in Leibniz' assertion that no two things are fully identical with each other. This then passes over into the basis for arithmetic's distinction between positive and negative numbers. The fact that contradiction can be shown to emerge from reflection on opposition does not mean, as Popper claims, that "Hegel's intention is to operate freely with all contradictions."[3] Rather our philosopher claims that any effort to analyze the surface features of anything to get at its essence will lead to contradictory results. And this contradiction generates the need for an explanation or ground. Not only does the law of non-contradiction hold. Because it holds, one must take seriously the nature of any contradiction that emerges from careful reflection if one is to have any success at all in discerning the underlying essence which it veils.[4]

Ground

Hegel then moves on to explore the various ways in which reflection thinks of the grounding relationship. One starts from the simple distinction between the essence as ground and its form as grounded; and this leads easily to the Aristotelian relation between matter as indeterminate potential and form as its determination. When reflection recognizes that the distinction between matter and form is really its own doing, then it thinks of their union as content in contrast to the form introduced by thought's own abstraction.

One now thinks of ground and grounded as in content the same, with only their form distinguishing them. But since the two are not really the same (else we would not have been led to distinguish essence from show), thought must be able to think what happens as the grounding relationship introduces real changes. In that scenario ground and grounded have identical content in some respects, while in others they are different. For a complete explanation, we must identify not only the way the two are identical, but what in addition introduces the differences.

We now have several factors combining to ground a single thing, each one functioning as a *condition* for the differentiated result: the original foundation, whatever is needed to motivate changes, what conspires to

---

3. See *The Open Society and its Enemies* (London: Routledge, 1966) II, 40.
4. Because both traditional and modern logics work with fixed logical constants and variables, they set aside the transitions of thought involved in analysis, implication and reflection. For these are dynamic, rather than static. Hegel's dialectic attempts to surmount this shortcoming by retaining the process in the understanding of its result. Thus it can see how one thought has led over to its opposite, creating a contradiction; and it recognizes that this contradiction, because it has arisen in some inevitable way, must be thoroughly explored to determine its ground.

bring them together into this peculiar synthesis. A condition, however, is not a complete ground. It is rather an immediate being which serves as only part of the material for a full process of grounding. And this process of grounding in turn is an immediate way of assembling an appropriate set of conditions to produce a grounded result. A complete ground, then, requires both the conditions and the relationship they have to each other. At first it might appear as if these various constituents function as immediate beings that are simply combined externally by some reflective act. But further reflection reveals that more is involved. For thought has shown that beings come to be and pass away; they are inherently transitory. Therefore immediate conditions never persist unaltered; and the grounding relationship can be understood as simply whatever dynamic of becoming occurs when a set of changing entities are brought together. When all the conditions are present, in other words, the grounded just comes to be. This whole pattern simply describes the nature of things.[5] As this nature of things works out its inherent process it emerges into existence.

In Hegel's analysis, two things have happened here. In the first place, the transitions of simple beings are now considered as a totality. This ability to consider all the moments together is the work of reflection. But in the second place reflective thought reaches this thought of the nature of things by showing that its own thinking activity in distinguishing ground from grounded is not an essential constituent of the dynamic. It has dissolved its own mediating role, and mutual reflection is built into the concepts being thought.

At the end of this whole development we have reached "existence." For what exists is the immediate being of what is essential. In this way Hegel has incorporated the traditional distinction between essence and existence. For the analysis of essence has led to the conclusion that, when fully worked out, the essential must come to be—it exists.

---

5. For this sense of "nature of things" Hegel adopts a German term, *Sache*, for which my dictionary offers as translations: "thing," "object," "matter," "legal case," "task," "business," "affair," "question," "subject," and "cause." I have at times been tempted to translate it as "heart of the matter," or "real thing." We have, in fact, encountered this concept earlier in the discussion of the measureless at the end of the Doctrine of Being. For, when Hegel revised this text in 1831, he introduced *Sache* to name the reality or "thing itself" that underlies the surface variation, and which becomes the absolutely indifferent. Here, in the second volume on Essence, we are back to his original text of 1813. The fact that *Sache* does not have a fixed place in the various editions of the *Encyclopaedia Logic* (1816, 1827, 1831) suggests that Hegel was intending to rework our present passage in his revision.

Chapter 10

Appearance

Existence

As we saw, the first section in the Doctrine of Essence ended with the thought of existence. In general speech, there is not much to distinguish "existence" from "being." But careful reflection may differentiate between the *pure* immediacy of whatever is, and "existence" as an immediate that has nonetheless emerged from some mediating process. Something essential emerges into existence. Hegel's analysis of "existence" involves exploring this paradoxical relationship between immediacy and mediation.

Whatever exists is a unit, distinguished from its environment. (Hegel uses the abstract expression "negative unity" for this state of affairs.) Therefore we do not have just "existence" in general, but "something existing"—what we would call "a thing." Further, to capture the tension between immediacy and mediation, we distinguish the essential "thing as it is in itself" from its inessential mediated existence. The former is an indeterminate unity, the latter develops a number of determinations whenever it is compared with others.

That existing multiplicity is not simply the product of some kind of external comparison. Each thing is what it is in virtue of the many ways by which it is different from others. In fact, this differentiation turns out to be essential; for, once the thing is abstracted from all determinations, there is nothing left with which we can identify it. In Hegel's example, the abstract "thing in itself" could be the library, the bookshelf, the book, or the page. We can distinguish between them only by taking account of the distinctive "properties" that identify each one.

Hegel compares this new concept, "property," with the concept of "quality" that surfaced in the Doctrine of Being. A "quality" is the way something is immediately determined, the way it loses the abstract emptiness of pure being. In contrast, a "property" belongs to a thing; it results from analyzing how a distinctive thing is to be identified. So a thing "has" properties. These determine what it is to be; and they continue to define it even as the surface qualities come and go. They are inherent powers that control what the surface existence looks like. And they come into play in various ways as the thing enters into interaction with other things in its environment.

What emerges from these considerations is paradoxical. We started by saying that the thing in itself is essential, and its existence is inessential. But now it turns out that the thing can only be distinguished from other things by its properties—by the distinctive contributions they make to the surface play of qualities. These properties are more important than the simple underlying thing. In fact, this thing is nothing more than the inessential collection of properties.

With this move, thought has begun to think of the properties as if they were things in their own right. Since they are not exclusive units, however, they are not so much things, as the material for things. A thing is made up of a range of materials, each one of which has the power to produce surface qualities when it interacts with other things. We could say that the "thing" is merely the locus where these properties come together. But that would leave aside that feature of "negative unity"—of being an exclusive unit—with which we began this reflection on "thing." At this point in our reflection, however, we can indicate that negative unity only by pointing it out—the thing is a "this" opposed to a "that."

"This" thing is made up of a collection of materials. But it is not simply identical with that collection. For a single thing could have some materials replaced by others, and yet remain the same "this." We have, then, a very puzzling combination of features. The distinctive materials combine to produce a thing, which is nonetheless a single, exclusive unity. These materials interact with materials in other things to produce a surface play of qualities. But the thing, which started out as the firm basis of existence, has dissolved into a mere collection of materials that is nonetheless exclusive—a "this" and not a "that." So the thing is in fact not what is essential. But neither are the materials or properties, for they can come and go without affecting the "thisness" of the thing. While one material cannot be where another is, they nevertheless interpenetrate within the porous unity of the thing. The sweetness, the whiteness, the crystalline texture are all equally present in every part of a cube of sugar, for all that they are quite distinct from one another. And the surface qualities vary as well, depending on how materials interact. Nothing is essential. The whole play of things, materials and qualities is simply the way reality appears. With this we have arrived at the next concept the logic needs to explore: "appearance."

Appearance

Whenever we call something "appearance," we are saying that its existence is mediated by something else—what could be called its negation. The underlying ground *appears*. But we know this ground as ground only because it refers to, and expresses itself as, this appearance. While each side—the ground and its appearance—is initially identified by this negative relation to its opposite, the ground has an additional positive sense, as that which persists even as appearances change. It is the simple identity underlying the transience of surface existence. We can say that it is the law which governs how things appear.[1] In other words, the realm of law is the peaceful ground underlying the turbulent world of appearance.

Law, with its schematic simplicity, can explain the patterns of appearance, but it leaves unexplained the changing content, which varies from case to case. Reflection on this state of affairs leads to a paradox. For law is to be the necessary ground of the inessential variety of existence. But this variety is itself essential, if the law is to find expression. As essential, it too must be grounded. In other words, it is not enough simply to explain the regular patterns that underlie the realm of appearance; we must also identify whatever grounds all its rich variation. This would seem to be a complete world, inherent and persisting in itself, which is the counterpart of the world that appears and explains the surface dynamic of changing existence. To constitute a full explanation of the whole realm of existence, this alternative realm must also be a totality; but because it is other than existence, as its negative counterpart, its content must be different from what is on the surface. Where one is white, the other is black; where one is good the other is evil. The underlying ground is an inverted world.[2]

Hegel's concept of the inverted world has continued to puzzled interpreters. But in its simplest form it can be understood as capturing a particular gambit that reflective thought has taken at times. Once science is no longer content to simply observe and classify the world of experience but seeks to discover its hidden secrets, it claims that the truth of existence is not found on the surface of things, but in some underlying reality which is the ground of appearance. The first step in this manœuvre is to look for the laws that remain constant, even as the givens of sense change and decay. And laws introduce a distinction between two features which are then related in a consistent way. Thus terrestrial gravity involves a ratio between distance and time. But when one wants to go beyond the simple formality of law to explain how and why things act the way they do,

---

1. Hegel is able to exploit a pun in the German. Appearance is posited (*gesetzt*) by the essential ground, which has turned out to be law (*Gesetz*).
2. This whole discussion in the *Logic* has been anticipated by the chapter on Understanding in the *Phenomenology*.

reflection may then suggest that reality is the inversion of appearance. In a magnet, the end which goes to the north is *in fact* its south pole; Something that looks white, because it includes all colours, is in fact black, because it reflects light and has nothing light in itself. Punishment for wrongdoing can look evil, but *in fact* it is a way of reconciling the criminal with society—a greater good. Hegel's concept of the inverted world is his way of explaining how and why we humans do at times develop explanations of this sort.

Reflective thought pushes further. What we have is the thought of two worlds which are identical in form and content, except that the content of one is the exact opposite, or inverse, of the other's. Each is defined by its relation to its counterpart; yet each is an independent whole. In such a reciprocal relationship one cannot really say that one is more essential, or more necessary, than the other. What is critical is this very relation itself. How is the whole related to itself as whole.

With this move we have gone beyond the distinction between inessential appearances and the essential world as it is in itself; we now want to identify as essential the relationship between the two worlds, when explaining why things are the way they are.

The Essential Relation

What kinds of relation provide this explanation? On the one hand each side of the relation is a totality, incorporating all that is. On the other hand they are not identical, but inversely related. Since a totality is a whole, the inverse of this "wholeness" would be the parts which make it up. So we have the relation between a whole and its parts. Each can be considered independently on its own; yet the whole can be a whole only because it incorporates the totality of the parts; and, were the parts abstracted from their relation to the whole, they would fall apart into a diverse multiplicity of beings. So, despite their independence, the two perspectives are related.

There is a problem. When we define the relation in this way we cannot say why the two sides are related. Considering a whole as a whole tells us nothing about why it must break up into parts; and considering the parts independently provides no indication of the way they are to be related within the whole. What we have is a tension between the implicit relation, and the supposed independence. We need, instead, a different kind of relation, where the more basic (what was the "whole") mediates and generates the other. This kind of relationship we can call "force and its expression."

"Force" captures the integrated, distinguished unity that is to be the underlying foundation; "expression" describes the multiplicity that results when such a force performs its distinguishing activity. But even this complex of concepts is not as simple as it seems to be at first. For a force, pure and simple, needs some kind of stimulation or circumstance to trigger its activity. And this impetus can only be derived from that environment where, in due course, it will produce its expressions. In other words, while force is supposed to be the initiator, it in turn must be initiated by the other side of the relation—the side that solicits the force and generates its activity. So the side that is to be the expression also functions as an initiating force; and the force that was to be basic is an expression of some alien solicitation. The two are reciprocally related in a play of forces which mutually trigger each other.

As something that is simple and immediate, force is finite; once we recognize that any force must itself be solicited by another force we enter into a self-constituting relationship, like that described earlier in Hegel's concept of the genuine infinite.[3] The dynamic activity is the inner core of what is going on; the multiple diversity is its external expression.[4] The essential, inverted relationship has now become that between inner and outer.

In this relationship the inner is what reflection identifies as essential, while the outer is simply the sphere of immediate being. Yet they are both identically the same reality.[5] The inner is the totality identified by reflection as essentially related to immediate being; the outer is this being, reflectively thought of as grounded in the intrinsic essence. Each is so closely identified with the other that we can hardly speak of any relation at all. Now that we have recognized that this "mutual relationship" is a single identity, we no longer retain the distinction between existence and essence, between appearance and things in themselves, or between one side and another of an essential relationship. We have something whose existence makes its essence actual—a reality which can be called "actuality."

It may seem that, in talking about essential relationships, Hegel has been playing with words. But there is an underlying strategy. He has been showing how many of the moves made by reflective thinkers when they have introduced distinctions like "whole/part," or "force/expression," or "inner/outer" to explain the world follow from the inherent meanings of the terms they are using. Each pair is designed to suggest independent states, but at the same time it contains meanings where each side implicates and requires the other. Those implicit implications shift as we move from one pair of terms to the next.

Thinkers, unable to distinguish the movement of pure thought from its concrete applications in both science and daily life, may confusedly think that the advances they are making result simply from the empirical evidence. Hegel is suggesting, instead, that they follow from the very complexity of

---

3. See Chapter 6.
4. Once again it is worth noting the pun: in German, "expression" is "*Äußerung*," "outer" or "external" is "*Äussere*."
5. Hegel's term here is "*Sache*," a term we have met several times before in both "Measure" and "Ground."

the terms being used—the distinctions that they are supposed to capture, and the relationships that are nonetheless inherent. Each of them, when analyzed into its components, turns out to be somewhat contradictory; and the resolution of that contradiction frequently leads on to new pairs of concepts that should resolve the difficulty. This, says Hegel, is the inevitable result whenever we use reflection to get at what is essential about the things we immediately encounter in the world. The thoughts we introduce to draw that distinction between surface and underlying ground have networks of connotation that complicate the issue; and these networks lead thought on, willy-nilly, to other related thoughts. What Hegel has done is expose how this kind of passage is grounded in the very activity of thought itself.

Chapter 11

Actuality

The Absolute

While Hegel calls this final section of the Doctrine of Essence "Actuality," he does not start out with this concept. For at the end of his discussion of essential relation, he has come to the concept of an identity which has dissolved any difference between the inner and the outer. Such an identity can simply be called "the absolute." This term is one adopted by Hegel's former colleague, Friedrich Schelling, to name that ultimate unity that incorporates into a single reality all that is. In this understanding, all determinations are dissolved in the absolute. The thought was not original with Schelling, however, for it had previously been developed by Spinoza, even though Spinoza had used the terms "god" or "nature," not "absolute," to name this all-encompassing identity.

The absolute is supposed to be a totality, incorporating the complete content of the whole. Any manifold is dissolved into its thoroughgoing unity. Were reflective thought to develop this concept of the absolute, it must show how all multiplicity and determination is ultimately dissolved within its identity. Any particular determinate reality is shown to be nothing other than the absolute itself. Whatever persistence it has depends on the absolute. So anything finite is completely transparent; its destiny is to disappear completely.

In such reflection—where we show how all determinations are, ultimately, evidence of the absolute—we always end with the absolute. But there is a problem. For our thought does not start from this radical identity but from some external multiplicity. If the absolute is to encompass everything that is, how can independent thought on its own, starting from its peculiar perspective, hope to understand this ultimate reality. We can resolve this difficulty only when we realize that, in this scenario, any reflection cannot be external to the absolute. Like any other determinate feature, it, too, must be related to the absolute as its origin and ground. So when it begins from external multiplicity, this must be some kind of exposition of the absolute itself.

The process of reflection, then, is not alien to, or external to, the absolute. It is rather an attribute of the absolute—a form it takes. We simply distinguish it, as a relative absolute, from the absolute-absolute (the expression is Hegel's). It contains the totality of that radical identity, but only under a particular determination. But if there is one determination, there is no reason why it cannot have others, so we have to think of the absolute as having an indeterminate number of such attributes.[1]

For all that each attribute is really the simple identity of the absolute, it nonetheless distinguishes out a variety of determinations, only to dissolve them again back into the absolute. Attributes can be differentiated from each other by the way and manner of this articulation—what could be called their modes. The modes, then, capture the full externality of the absolute, even though they are going to be reabsorbed by that absolute to ensure that it remains a simple identity.

Strangely enough, while we started with the absolute as a pure and simple identity, it now turns out that it can be genuinely thought of as an identity only to the extent that it is understood as dissolving all the diversity of the modes back into this identity. For without the modes, there would be nothing to identify. As a result we find that we have moved in a circle: from absolute identity through attribute and mode back to absolute identity. When we think about it, then, the absolute is nothing but this dynamic circular movement. The abstract, static and pure identity with which we started is a mere abstraction of thought. The development through attributes and modes is the way the absolute manifests itself. It is the way it moves from abstract isolation to actuality.

Actuality

Hegel starts his discussion of this concept by contrasting it with "being" and with "existence." "Being" covers anything that is, without qualification. "Existence" is distinguished from its essence. The "actual," however, includes the sense that its essence has been actualized; this essence, however, is now called "possibility."[2]

"Possibility" has a double sense. On the one hand it is related to, but different from, the actual. On the other hand it affirms that the actual is self-identical; anything that is possible must not be self-contradictory. In this latter sense, though, any number of things, considered on their own, are possible, since each is identical with itself. Yet, were we to combine them,

---

1. Spinoza says there are an indefinite number of attributes, but he identifies only two: thought and extension.
2. A paragraph by paragraph exposition of this section of the *Science of Logic* can be found in "The Necessity of Contingency," *Hegel on Logic and Religion* (Albany: SUNY, 1992) 39–51.

we would find contradictions: it is possible that my next pet will be a goldfish; and it is possible that my next pet will be a hamster; but it is impossible for my next pet to be a hamster-goldfish.

Once this has been made clear we realize that we have to rethink our concept of "actual." It needs to include the sense of *actualizing* one possibility among several. The resulting actual could be called "the contingent," since it could have been otherwise. On the other hand, it could also be called "the necessary," for once it has become actual, the other possibilities have been excluded: it cannot then be otherwise. This sense of "necessity" is, however, rather formal and abstract, just like the previous senses of "actuality" and "possibility."

Reflective thought does not stop here. For what distinguishes one possibility from others is the particular way it is determined. So when we have an actual that realizes one possibility among several we have an actual defined as having determinate properties. We could call this a "real" actual.

Starting from this sense of "actual" we find that we need to adjust our sense of "possible." For the possible that underlies a particular determination is its real possibility—the condition that enables it to become actual. Since any actual has many determinations, it is the result of a number of such conditions. Each condition starts out simply as one given actuality; but it becomes a possibility once it conspires with others to produce a new actual.

On its own, one isolated condition (or possibility) cannot produce the concrete actual. A number must come together and be combined. Only when this happy conjunction occurs does that actual become *really* possible. But this has a peculiar consequence. For once all the relevant conditions are present the possible *must* become actual; it cannot persist as mere possibility. Relative to these particular conditions, the actual has become necessary. It is, then, a relative necessity, contingent on the peculiar circumstances of a distinctive situation.

We now have a very complex picture. We have a number of actuals which, when they combine in certain ways, become the real possibility for other actuals. In that larger picture we find both contingency and necessity, for it is a contingent matter which particular actuals are given; but once they are present and associated in appropriate ways, certain results necessarily happen. This picture as a whole gives us a new sense of "actuality." For we are now using it to name whatever is, as this total network of conditions. Since there is nothing else to be considered, we can call it "absolute actuality."

This sense of "actual" requires an adjustment in our sense of "possible." For if everything is included in the former, there is nothing distinctive which could define the latter. There is no answer to the question: "Why is there anything at all? Why not nothing?" But this leads again to a paradox: what was supposed to be intrinsically necessary is radically contingent, for there is no ground that can explain why this absolute actuality is what it is.

We resolve this paradox by reflecting on how we reached it. The absolutely actual is the total interplay of real actualities and real possibilities. If we think of these, not as independent terms in their own right, but as components of the whole, we notice that within the absolutely actual there must be distinct actualities, and these must combine to become the possibility of other actualities. We need to have clear distinct entities, but we also need to have intrinsic relations by which they lead one to another. In fact, this is the way actuality is. With this Hegel has moved beyond formal actuality, real actuality and even absolute actuality to "the actual," pure and simple. And it is this internal network of distinctions and relations that constitutes its possibility. This dynamic is the way the actual determines itself. As self-causing, or self-constituting, this actual is absolutely necessary; it is its own ground.

The sense of "necessity" we have now reached involves the internal relations that constitute the actual. We are no longer talking about the essential relations by which existence appears, which we discussed in the previous chapter. We are talking about the necessary relationships that make reality what it is. So we move on from discussing "actuality" as such to talking about these kinds of "absolute relation."

Absolute Relation

The final sense of "necessity" we reached was of that process by which the actual constitutes itself. Distinctions are introduced and then resolved. We are thinking, then, of the kind of being which generates itself—a concept for which we have the name "substance." The process by which substance constitutes itself involves a coming to be and a passing away, with elements, not themselves essential, being posited as distinctive. The totality of this surface show, as distinct from the underlying substantiality, is the realm of accidentality.

When we turn to think about the relationship between substance and its accidents, we recognize that the latter is the way the former actualizes itself. That is to say, for all the dynamic flux of the surface, it is the underlying substance which on the one hand creates the various accidental moments, and on the other hand destroys them. Indeed, creation inevitably destroys what was there before, and destruction opens the way for creation. So, even though accidents appear to exercise influence over each other, it is really the power of the substance that makes all these things happen—giving one more value than another, so that its possibility comes to be actual and forces the other actual to disappear into mere possibility.

Further reflection, however, notices that the substance can only be substance to the extent that it does acquire the form of accidentality. Its inherent power needs to be revealed in that dynamic flux. Equally, the realm of accidentality is inherently substance; when one accident disappears and is replaced by another, this simply is the way the substantial power works itself out. With this thought of a power working to produce a result we have moved from the language of substance to the language of cause.

Hegel takes us through three stages in his analysis of "cause." Initially we think of cause as original and originating—the process by which a substance becomes actual.[3] But a cause can be a cause, only to the extent that it has an effect. Once the effect has come to be, it is no longer a cause— nor is the effect any longer an effect, but only another thing. In other words, the cause is extinguished *as cause* once it has done its work; and the effect is extinguished as effect, once it has fully come to be. When we think about cause as a strictly formal relationship, we come up with this paradoxical result.

This leads, then, to Hegel's second stage, or determinate causality in contrast with formal causality. Here we think of causality as only one aspect of a determinate substance, so that it can continue to be, once the effect has been produced. Similarly the effect is simply a change in the determination of another substance which, in other respects, persists through the change. The cause, then, is simply some specific content that is simply passed from the cause to the effect. For example (says Hegel), some pigment causes the colour in an object, or wet rain dampens the street. This kind of causal analysis is really a form of tautology, where the cause and the effect are really the same thing, but associated with different substances.

To avoid this kind of banality, causal analysis takes another tack. We want the cause to be different from the effect. But this means that the causing substance can only work because the substance to be altered allows it to happen. We often say that the climate of a certain region *causes* the distinctive characteristics of its population; or that a draught *causes* a cold, but we have here surrendered any necessity. For these "causes" are not what MAKES the result happen. Anything that is living or anything that involves a social dynamic responds to originating influences and determines to what extent they can work their wiles.

What we have, then, are two (or more) things, each having an independent existence. For one to become a cause, it must be stimulated to take action. But this means that there must be a further cause which triggers its causal activity. So we end up with an infinite regress of causes, as each new cause must itself be stimulated to act. Similarly when we look the other way, we see that, when a cause works on an effect, it introduces a change, which in its turn makes that thing into a cause. In other words, every cause is itself an effect, and every effect becomes a cause.

---

3. Another pun: Hegel takes delight in the fact that, in German, actual (*Wirklich*), effect (*Wirkung*), and to work (*Wirken*) share the same root.

This conclusion is the result of reflection on what happens when independent things are considered as both causes and effects. But whenever we have an infinite regress we have a reciprocal movement from one concept to another and back again. And we move beyond the bad infinity of repetition only by considering how these two concepts are in fact related to each other. What happens when we consider in detail just what happens between cause and effect.

In Hegel's third stage, causality presupposes certain conditions—what he calls conditioned causality. First, there must be some passive substance to act upon, quite distinct from the cause, or active substance. Second, the cause must change itself so that it can work; it must shift from being simply an independent being to being an agent. So in a certain sense it is itself a passive substance. Third, the passive substance is not completely passive. For it provides the conditions that incite the cause to work in the first place. In other words it also is effective, and acquires causal force. So it is equally an active substance.

Where we have two substances, each of which acts on the other, and each of which receives the action of the other, we have a pattern of action and reaction. There is a reciprocal dynamic which moves beyond the linear regress of finite cause to a more comprehensive mutuality of interaction. Hegel is here making the move from Kant's analysis of cause in the *Critique of Pure Reason* to his analysis of organic teleology in the *Critique of Judgement*. He shows that this shift is not simply a contingent feature of regulative thinking, but inherent in the concept of cause itself. Kant, to be sure, anticipates this move by including reciprocity in his table of categories, but he never develops its implications in the way he does with substance and cause.

To move forward, we need to recall the context of this whole discussion of substance, cause and reciprocity. These concepts have emerged as ways in which a totality is related to itself—what Hegel has called absolute relation. And this totality is the actual, as the determinate way whatever is— the absolute—articulates itself.

The concept of actuality itself emerged from a discussion of how essence shows itself to be. The actual is what realizes its essence, having transcended the distinction between the essential and the inessential, between essence and existence, between appearance and the thing in itself. Now the actual has turned out to be a dynamic of mutual interaction in which each of its moments is both active and passive with respect to each other moment. And that reciprocity binds the whole together into a distinctive unity.

Hegel stresses the importance of reciprocal interaction, for it captures an essential moment of the whole preceding analysis. Being and nothing reciprocally interact in the concept of becoming, as do finite and the beyond in the concept of infinity, quantity and quality in the concept of measure, essential and inessential in the concept of reflection, identity and difference in contradiction and ground, existence and appearance in the concept of actuality. As we have seen, it is a key feature of the critical move Hegel calls sublation, or *Aufheben*. In all of these cases, however, we have a distinction between the processes which think the concepts and those concepts themselves. But now the content being thought identifies and articulates the mutual interaction implicit in the process of sublation. The difference between the thought that is doing the thinking and the thought that is being thought has collapsed. Both have the same dynamic.

Throughout the *Logic*, thought has found itself led into new thoughts whenever it has focused on a concept. Gradually it has brought these moves forward to centre stage where they can be identified conceptually: the dialectical transitions of becoming; the synthetic determinations of reflection. We have now introduced the final, and most critical, move into the spotlight. This function (as Kant calls it) occurs when we have a double transition—a reciprocal interaction. The whole self-contained movement collapses into a unity that incorporates all its components and is thus uniquely defined in contrast with other such concepts. This process Kant calls "conceiving." Once we identify what conceiving involves, we will have self-reflexively (and self-reflectively) thought about the very thinking we are doing.

In every pattern of mutual interaction we have a totality which incorporates its constituent moments while cancelling their independence. By encompassing this variety into a single whole, it functions as a universal. When this complex synthesis collapses into a distinctive unity and is isolated negatively from the reasoning that led up to it, we have something singular. And as the simple unity of universality and discreteness, it is particular. In other words, it is what Kant had called a concept. For a concept is a singular thought which, though universal, determines itself in the very act of conceiving, defining its particular moments and features. With this shift, Hegel concludes the second book of his *Science of Logic* on Essence, and prepares to consider conceptual thought as such—Kant's discursive functions of unity or concepts. And, following Kant, he investigates their critical role in the formation of logical judgements and arguments. So we have set the stage for the next book in Hegel's *Logic*: The Doctrine of the Concept.

PART IV

The Doctrine of the Concept

Chapter 12

Concept and Judgement

Conceiving

Concepts are functions—acts of conceiving. They unite into an immediate thought the syntheses that reflection has brought together.[1] Hegel has reached this stage in the logical development by way of the thought of reciprocity: where each moment produces, yet presupposes, its counterpart, generating an intimate togetherness. Conceiving integrates this synthesis into a unity. Because it incorporates a number of moments into its own simplicity, it is comprehensive and universal. This universality is not an abstraction, common to a number of particulars but unrelated to their mutual differences. Rather it includes the various moments of its integrating dynamic, and to that extent is both determinate (and so particular) and distinctive (and so singular).

As dynamic thinking activity, conceiving focuses on this element of determination, thinks of alternative possible determinations, and then unites the original universal with its contrary species into a more comprehensive, generic universal. At this point in the analysis, that higher universal is still not an abstract genus, but rather remains a self-determining dynamic incorporating the various subordinate moments within its own integrity.

Conceiving, then, is an intellectual activity in which self-conscious life (or, in Hegel's language, "spirit") articulates the integrated sense of its own self-constituting dynamic. Since that dynamic is nothing but the way spirit's determinate moments mutually influence each other, however, we need to identify the particular character of that reciprocal interaction. For each act of integrating a thought into a concept is made determinate by the content integrated.

We have met determinations before. In the doctrine of being, a determination is a simple quality that emerges whenever we think of a being; in essence, reflection uses determinations to distinguish the

---

1. Recall here the discussion of Kant in Chapter 3.

essential from the inessential. Now, in the context of conceiving, a determination makes a universal something distinctive. Even though it follows from the internal content of the concept, this conceptual determination can also be used to distinguish this thought from other universals. In other words, within the logic of the concept, the determination particularizes the universal. So we can now distinguish between the concept's universality and its determinate particularity.

With this move we have two distinct moments: the concept's determination—its particularity—and its comprehensive universality. Once they have been distinguished in this way, the two terms function as particulars vis-à-vis each other, even though one of the particulars is called the universal. What marks them out as particulars is that they are distinguished from each other within a more general context. By focusing on this moment of difference we are led to significant implications. For now the universal moment is no longer comprehensive, but separated from its determinate content. It has become abstract, for it now excludes this other determinate moment and has become indifferent to it. The act of conceiving inevitably leads to abstractions.

Usually when people talk of determinate concepts they are referring to such abstract universals. The kind of thinking that fixes the meanings of such abstractions and proceeds to work with them as unalterable units is called understanding. Frequently that is as far as conventional thinking goes. For, moulded by the mechanistic assumptions of the seventeenth and eighteenth century, we assume that things are to be explained by reducing them to the static components out of which they are constructed. According to Hegel's analysis, however, such abstract units are not the foundation of all thinking, but the result of the act of conceiving. They emerge when thinking concentrates on its own dynamic, identifies its internal distinctions and distinguishes them as independent terms.

If abstractions are not the first word, though, they are also not the last. For Hegel says that understanding's "infinite power" of separating concrete terms into their abstract determinations and then grasping the depth of their differences leads over dialectically to contrary concepts. Nonetheless, understanding's process of abstraction is necessary, for it is the only way reason can grasp the structure of its own thoughts. In other words, while the immediate transitions of becoming are parallel to dialectical reason, and reflection is the counterpart to speculative reason, it is in the particularizing, or determining, activity of conceptual thought where understanding finds its place.[2]

Particularizing, then, is the process of abstraction—of understanding. But when thought pushes this process to its extreme, it leaves behind any consideration of what connects one particular to another. It focuses simply

---

2. Compare *EL* §§79–82.

on this unique unit, which is no longer thought as one particular over against another, both subsumed under an implicit universal. We are rather thinking something singular; having abandoned any use of universal descriptions we simply refer to it as unique.[3]

Once we turn to "the singular" we find that it plays a number of functions. In the first place the abstract universal, although universal in form, is singular in content. In the second place, the two earlier particulars which were distinguished as universal and particular concepts can be read as a set of distinct terms, to which singularity can be added as a third, equivalent member. In other words, when conceiving fully determines the constituent moments of its content it distinguishes universal, particular and singular as three objects of reference, all equally singular.

In the third place, singularity results in the break up of the concept. For the singular is referred to as a unit that excludes all universality—as a "this" that is simply related to itself. It stands radically opposed to any abstract concept, even though the act of reference, by which it is indicated, results from conceptual thought annulling its own comprehensive inclusiveness. This means, however, that any singular implicitly refers to the abstract universal from which it has been separated. To articulate how universal and singular, though radically different, are nonetheless implicitly connected, thought adopts the use of propositions (or judgements).[4]

Hegel has thus set the stage for his discussion of the formal logic of his day—the various types of judgement and forms of inference. He has done so by showing that comprehensive thought, in defining its own determinations, has to separate, and thus abstract, the universal from the determinate; and whatever is so determinate that no universal remains becomes the singular object of reference. Since the particular, though determinate, continues to be conceptual, it will be able to serve within the syllogism as a bridge between the two extremes. But all three moments of universal, particular and singular have lost that dynamic completeness with which

---

3. While Hegel has sections titled "Universal Concept" and "Particular Concept," the third section is simply called "The Singular." The distinctive uniqueness of the concept is collapsed into something that can no longer be thought conceptually but simply indicated. It needs to be noted, however, that in the later *Encyclopaedia Logic* Hegel claims that a totality considered as a unity is also called the singular. The argument he sketches there thus varies from the one advanced here, which follows the larger *Science of Logic*. It is the ability of conceiving to abstract from universal connections and thus focus strictly on a singular which has been operative throughout Hegel's logic in the move which he calls *Aufhebung*, when understanding takes a reciprocal movement and "collapses" it into a unity. The universality involved in the movement back and forth from "being" to "nothing" or from "cause" to "effect" is set aside and the intellect directs its attention to the resulting self-contained thought as an unmediated singular.

4. Hegel again plays on words, for the German word for judgement—*Urteil*—could be read as "primordial division." For all that the terms of a proposition are distinct, they were nonetheless originally connected.

conceptual thinking began, and have become fixed individuals, each with its own determinate content; as a result they now serve as the constituent terms of judgements and syllogisms. These the *Logic* now goes on to explore.

Judging

The most basic kind of proposition simply couples a singular with an abstract universal: the affirmative judgement "Socrates is human" or "S is P." This judgement, however, does not capture the fact that the singular as singular is quite different from the universal as abstract. To express that difference we need a negative judgement: "the singular is not a universal" or "S is not P."

Negations are the way we determine a thought and distinguish it from its contraries. In negative judgements the "not" applies to the predicate, implying that it is one particular among several and that the subject is in fact related to one of the others.[5] The radical difference between the irreducible singularity of the subject and the conceptuality of the universal predicate, then, has not been captured by this form of negation. One needs instead to apply the "not" to the copula rather than to the predicate. The result is what traditional logicians have called the infinite judgement: "it is not the case that S is P." For examples Hegel provides: "Spirit is not alkaline," and "the rose is not an elephant."

Even when it is true, an infinite judgement imparts little, if any, information; so we need to look back at the connection between subject and predicate in these basic sentences to see how it can be made more instructive. In the first place, the predicate as a bare abstract universal is too empty. If we were to incorporate some of the implications of the negative judgement, and adopt as predicate a universal that includes contrary particulars—a category or class—it would contribute more to the connection asserted in the judgement. Once this is done, the copula (or connection between subject and predicate) does not simply assert an identity or a difference; it rather says that the subject is included under, or subsumed by, the predicate class. The subject, then, becomes a singular existent. The resulting judgement in traditional logic would still read "S is P"—"the singular is universal," but its meaning is more precisely defined as a statement of membership in a class: "This is a member of the class C," or more simply the singular judgement; "this is P." We have moved from judgements of quality to judgements of quantity, or (as Hegel calls them) judgements of reflection.

---

5. This type of negation was used by Carnap and Ryle when they defined category words: saying "this A is not blue" places A under the category of coloured.

A singular "this" does not fully capture the universality of the class that functions as predicate, so one indicates that the subject could be more general by including others, using a particular judgement: "Some S are P." But just as the thought of "something" led over to the thought of "something else,"[6] the particular judgement suggests its counterpart: "Some (other) S are not P." The subject term on its own includes both sets—those that are P and those that are not P. As a result we find ourselves thinking not only of all the subjects ("some" and "the others"), but we once again have a more encompassing universal or class that includes both P and not P. So one is led to a universal judgement: "All S are U."

Just as, at the end of the discussion of the judgements of quality, the abstract predicate comes to be defined more precisely as a category with particular species, so in the judgements of reflection the subject has expanded from being an indicated singular to being all of a conceptually defined set. This means that one can now think of a judgement in which two universals—two concepts—are coupled, not as a simple association, nor as membership in a class, but as necessarily related. This is what traditional logic has called a categorical judgement. Although it may have the same form as an affirmative judgement—"S is P"—it presupposes a different content. In an affirmative judgement an abstract universal is simply said to inhere in a singular subject: "this rose is red"; in a categorical judgement a class is incorporated into its broader genus: "the rose is a plant." So we moved on to judgements of relation (in Hegel's terms, judgements of necessity).

Because of the ambiguity that remains in the form of the categorical judgement, it does not adequately express its essential conditions. For it is supposed to affirm the necessary connection between the two concepts; but it does not differ from a simple affirmative statement. To make the implicit necessity explicit, one needs to adopt a different judgement form, where the necessary link is actually expressed: the hypothetical judgement "if S then P." The copula or connection has now shifted from being the simple verb "to be" to showing how a condition grounds the conditioned by means of an "if-then."

Such hypothetical judgements do capture the way a subject necessarily leads over to the predicate, but it leaves undefined what it is about the antecedent which makes the move necessary. Anything could be slotted into this form as long as the appropriate sequence is maintained.[7] What

---

6. See Chapter 6.
7. As more recent logic has shown, valid formal hypotheticals may include not only contrary-to-fact conditionals such as "if the moon is made of green cheese, then I'm a monkey's uncle" but also such strange statements as "if day regularly follows night, then 2+2=4."

thought really requires is a judgement form that captures the way one specific concept requires others. The appropriate form for this is the disjunctive judgement: "A is B or C or D," which carries the attendant sense: "A includes B and C and D."

If qualitative judgements defined the predicate more precisely and quantitative judgements focused on the subject, the judgements of necessity—categorical, hypothetical and disjunctive—have refined the way they are connected to each other. In a disjunction both subject and predicate are universal—the subject as a comprehensive concept, the predicate as an exhaustive listing of its particular species. Yet their identity is simply given as a categorical assertion. It does not state the necessity of their relationship. So Hegel moves on to the kinds of judgement that define the mode of the coupling relation—the judgements of modality or (again following Hegel) judgements of the concept.

A simple assertion does not provide any warrant for why it should be said. It is a singular intellectual act, and cannot do justice to the universality of the subject that is supposed to determine the appropriate predicate. Since, as Kant argued, universals are possibles, not actuals, that universality could better be captured by a problematic judgement: "S is possibly P."

No sooner is that expedient tried than thought recognizes its inadequacy. For what is only possibly P could equally well be not P. Pure possibility does not discriminate between them. So what is needed is a judgement form that does justice to the necessity involved in the universal: "S must be P."

With this Hegel has completed his analysis of the traditional forms of judgement. He has shown that conceptual thought, in order to articulate its own assumptions, must construct ever more inclusive judgement forms. But the process does not stop here, for the simple assertion of a necessary coupling does not show the reason for that necessity. To make that rationale explicit one must move beyond judgement to inference, where a middle term justifies our connecting subject to predicate. So Hegel now turns to a discussion of syllogisms.

Chapter 13

Syllogism

The Syllogism of Determinate Being

In the judgement of necessity, "S must be P," we refer not only to the subject and the predicate but to the necessity of their relationship. To justify this necessity we require some mediating term that is related to both the subject and the predicate. The subject is referred to as the topic of the sentence—a singular; the predicate is a general universal; the middle term, then, must share both the concrete determinacy of the subject and the universality of the predicate, so it functions as a particular. As a result, the first form of syllogism is one where a particular mediates between something considered as a singular and something considered as a universal.

In the very early stages of the *Logic*[1] a transition or becoming is identified as the basic link that connects two concepts. In a similar way, the most elementary kind of connection that could make an inference necessary involves two transitions, first from the singular to the particular, and then from the particular to the universal. The conclusion simply collapses these two transitions into a single one— from singular to universal. Its form is the classical Barbara syllogism: "John is tall; tall things are sublime; so John is sublime."

The problem with this kind of reasoning is that singular subjects can have any number of particular determinations; and universals include any number of particulars, so it is entirely contingent which syllogism one constructs. By choosing a different description of the singular subject, and then selecting an appropriate universal for that middle term we can reach the exact opposite conclusion: "John is petulant; petulant things are abhorrent; so John is abhorrent."

The reason for this paradox is that the immediate transitions which form the connections in the premises simply occur as singular events. In other words what is really mediating the inference is not the particular concept but something that just happens to be the case.

---

1. The Doctrine of Being.

To capture this kind of inferential mediation we need a different kind of syllogistic form—one in which a unique singular serves as a middle term between particular and universal. In this second kind of syllogism the major premise is formally the same as the conclusion of the first: a singular is conjoined to a universal through a simple transition. The minor premise, however, poses a problem. For one cannot simply pass over from a particular to a singular, and so the inference cannot function transitively. Instead one must simply affirm that the two are in fact associated—that the particular happens to describe the singular. The contingency in that association allows the syllogistic form to retain the convention that the singular is the natural subject, for one can equally say that the singular happens to be particular: "Some S is P." This then means that the conclusion as well can only be a particular judgement: "Some S are U." The result is what Aristotle called the third syllogistic figure, Datisi: "Dogs are animals, some dogs are noisy; so some noisy things are animals."[2]

The novelty in this syllogism is the connection between the singular and the particular. This does not involve an immediate transition, but rather a reflective synthesis or association. The two descriptions are simply conjoined. But a conjunction which contains two component particulars is a kind of universal, although a very bare, abstract one. Nonetheless since it has been identified as the problematic core of the second kind of inference, its mediating role needs to be identified by an appropriate syllogistic form: one in which a universal mediates between a singular and a particular.

In the first premise of this kind of syllogism the particular is associated with the universal (which has the form of the conclusion of the second syllogism); in the second premise the singular is connected by an intellectual transition with the universal (which replicates the conclusion of the first syllogism). Because both the singular and the particular are associated with the same universal, the inference is that they can be associated with each other. However, as we have seen, the universal is connected to the particular not because of any intrinsic relationship but because of some arbitrary, synthetic association. So the universal is left quite indeterminate and abstract. Lacking any intrinsic conceptual relationship, the universal and the particular have no positive association; they can only be distinguished negatively. So the first premise must be negative. And since this exclusion defines the universal's mediating role the negative feature must be carried through to the conclusion. So we have Aristotle's second figure, Cesare: "Flowers are not dogs; spaniels are dogs; so spaniels are not flowers."[3]

---

2. By converting the minor premise to "some noisy things are dogs," this becomes Darii of the first figure.

3. By converting the major premise to "No dogs are flowers" we have Celarent of the first figure. Hegel notes that the only thing we need to generate what traditional logic has called the fourth figure is the conversion of the negative and particular conclusions in the second and third figure.

With this third kind of syllogism, the formalism of the traditional syllogism becomes explicit. For the universal that makes it work is a bare abstraction that excludes all determinate qualities. The fullest expression of how these empty generalities function can be found in the mathematical formula, "If two things are equal to the same thing, they are equal to each other," for here the three terms are abstracted from all qualitative characteristics and considered only in terms of their magnitude. No conceptual reasoning is involved at all.

On the one hand, then, this analysis of the traditional syllogism results in a bare formalism which can tell us nothing about the determinate nature of conceptual thinking. But thought is not limited to considering the final stage of its series of inferential moves. It can reflect on them as a whole to see if there is some kind of basic principle that is implicit and essential. From this perspective one notices that the three syllogisms make a set, for each of the three conceptual determinations—particular, singular, and universal— mediates the coupling of the other two, with the result that, in a strictly formal sense, the syllogisms justify each other's premises.

On the other hand, since the reasoning is formal, the mediated connection asserted in the conclusion must in fact be grounded in some immediate association. Reflecting on this, thought recognizes that any effective inferential mediation cannot simply abstract from all qualitative determination but must incorporate immediate concrete content. And such content can only be provided by referring to singulars, which are both qualitatively determined, and can be counted as members of some universal class. One needs this concrete content to establish something more than a purely formal link between the two terms of the conclusion.

The Syllogism of Reflection

Hegel now returns to the three patterns for the syllogism and reconstructs them, taking into account this new requirement. In the form where particularity mediates, the particular mediating quality must be such that it specifies its individual instantiations. In addition to being predicated of a singular subject in the minor premise, then, it explicitly collects all of the individuals it describes in the major: All M is P; S is M; so S is P.

This inference, which Hegel calls the syllogism of allness is, however, redundant. For if we say that all plants receive nutrition continuously, and that this holly bush is a plant, then we do not introduce anything new when we conclude that this holly bush receives its nutrition continuously. That fact has already been mentioned in the major premise.

The real question posed by this form of syllogism is how we are justified in making the claim that all plants receive their nutrition continuously. For this we need a different kind of inference—induction—which (like Hegel's second figure) uses singulars, or a limited set of them, to establish the universality of the connection between a particular class and its abstract quality. Because a finite set of individuals are both plants and receive nutrition continuously we infer that all plants are characterized in this way.

This inference builds on the distinction between the finite set of plants that serve as its middle term and the complementary set of plants not mentioned there, but included in the "all" of the conclusion. Implicit in the reasoning is the assumption that what applies to some applies to all. But much earlier in the logic of "something," we found that our natural inference is not from some to "all" but rather to something other with different qualities that becomes its contrary.[4] A similar shift posed a problem for the particular judgement. There is, then, a basic contingency in induction, because there is no necessity when we extend a specific quality from the finite set selected for the premise to the complementary set that needs to be included in the conclusion. Yet induction assumes that the two sets are for all practical purposes identical.

Another inference is required to make this assumption explicit: an argument from analogy. In this form of inference what is known to apply to one set of individual plants, for example, is extended to other plants. Because these trees and bushes and grasses are green, then we assume that other plants, like mushrooms, will also be green. As this example shows, however, although analogical inferences are essential to the inductive extension of a predicate from a finite set to the whole class, they are themselves radically contingent. For one has no way of knowing whether the predicate one selects is essential to the class, or only contingently related to the items enumerated.

What underlies the inferences of allness, induction and analogy—which Hegel calls syllogisms of reflection—is their reliance on singular instances as their mediating term, either gathered together in a set, or taken as an individual. Since singulars, as objects of reference, are explicitly distinguished from the abstract universals used to characterize them, there can be no necessity that would legitimate any inference to new conclusions. These singulars provide only an external synthesis of the two extremes they are meant to mediate. What thought needs to effect a genuine mediation to something new is a universal concept—the kind of thought that both defines its particular determinations, and indicates the singulars to which it applies. This requires a different kind of inference—a kind Hegel calls syllogisms of necessity.

The Syllogism of Necessity

The first kind of inference that uses a fully determinate concept as the middle term is a categorical syllogism. This has the same form as both the Barbara syllogism and the inference of allness, but it is given a different content. The middle term is a substantial genus—"human" for example—the predicate

---

4. See Chapter 6.

is an abstract characterization of this genus; and the subject is one of its singular instances: "Socrates is human; humans are mortal; so Socrates is mortal."

While the content of this inference grounds its necessity, its form still retains an element of contingency. For the singular subject, as well as the abstract universal predicate, are named independently, as if on their own they had an unmediated being. As immediate they would have determinations other than the one specified in the middle term, which would allow them to be incorporated into other such syllogisms. In other words, the syllogistic form does not capture the necessity of the inference.

We need an argument form which explicitly expresses the necessary connection and the way it relates the independent terms. This would be modus ponens (Hegel calls it a hypothetical syllogism) in which the major premise is a hypothetical judgement: If A then B. This form of proposition asserts a necessary relationship without requiring the independent existence of its terms. The minor premise asserts that the antecedent, A, also has an independent existence, so that it is both mediating and immediate. B in the conclusion has been mediated by the inference, but is also ascribed immediate existence. "If coral is a living thing then it will grow; coral is a living thing; so it grows."

This syllogism states that a necessary relationship has been given determinate being. But the counterpart of this claim is that the inference as a whole is simply a different way of expressing the necessary relationship that was given in the hypothetical premise. The unity of that statement is simply broken apart by the syllogism into its independent constituents, a kind of activity that Hegel calls a negative unity.

Not only does the categorical syllogism have a form that does not express the necessity of its inferential content; the same applies to modus ponens. For affirmed as immediate existents, the minor premise and the conclusion fail to indicate the mediating relationship which they nonetheless presuppose and require. A fully adequate syllogistic form will show how each term is implicitly involved in every other one. This is captured in the disjunctive syllogism: "The expected precipitation will be either rain, sleet or snow; it will be too cold for rain and too warm for snow; so the expected precipitation will be sleet."[5]

In this syllogism the major premise says that the universal is exhaustively defined in its constituent species. The minor says that the universal is an exclusive singular. The conclusion affirms that it is a member of a particular species. In other words it explicitly states the way a universal concept—a "discursive function of unity," as Kant would say—is defined as made up of its constituent particulars; then it goes on, as a distinctive singular, to exclude some of the options. Rather than being an inference to

---

5. Hegel also uses a form of exclusive disjunction: "The expected precipitation will be either rain, sleet or snow; it turned out to be snow; so it is neither rain nor sleet."

something new, this syllogism simply articulates the nature of conceptual thought in and of itself.

By taking all these reflections together and integrating them into a single thought, Hegel can generate a new immediate concept. Thinking now moves beyond the subjectivity of a form distinguished from its content. Having formally articulated its own nature, it has become objective. In other words thought is now conceiving something immediate that is fully in and of itself. With this inference, Hegel has shifted to the concept of objectivity—of that which is the complementary counterpart of the subjective dynamic of conceiving.

Before tracing the final sections of Hegel's *Logic* it is worth our while to reflect on what he has been doing in this discussion of concept, judgement and syllogism. The various forms that he explores are not his creation. Rather he has incorporated the traditional table of judgements, as well as the full range of standard inferences, into a systematic pattern. So Hegel is not proposing a new logic. He is rather offering a philosophy of traditional logic: showing, first of all, how our conceiving sets the conditions for any discussion of reasoning by distinguishing singular objects of reference from abstract universals; and then showing why each judgement form and type of syllogism is introduced in turn to capture a relation or inference presupposed, but only implicitly, in the previous form. The key transitions— from judgements of quality to judgements of quantity, or from formal syllogisms to induction and analogy—exploit the peculiar function of speculative reason—looking back on the previous moves as a whole, noticing a necessary feature that has disappeared in the interval, and then synthetically incorporating this into a new, more comprehensive perspective.

In his analysis of each form, he shows how its limitations become exposed when we consider all its implications. In the subsequent form we learn how those weaknesses have been resolved. This philosophical analysis of formal logic, then, starts by simply trying to understand a form as it is, without any mediating framework. By exposing its faults we are led into contrary and complementary considerations through the process Hegel calls dialectical reason. And the reflective synthesis of the different descriptions that makes possible a new beginning is the work of speculative reason. Thus the stage is set for the conceptual integration that produces a new unified concept, which in its turn can be understood apart from all mediation.[6]

---

6. In *On Hegel's Logic* (Atlantic Highlands, NJ: Humanities Press, 1981) I made a first attempt at reconstructing Hegel's analysis to show how the various forms of symbolic logic can be derived, moving from the conjunction of a function with a singular, to membership in a class to propositional forms, and then how this can become expanded into a) a formal variation of the Aritotelian syllogisms, b) modern induction and analogy, and c) the basic inferences of propositional calculus. On rereading, I have become aware that this project needs to be reworked in detail, although I suspect it is still feasible.

Subjective conceiving, then, is the process by which self-reflective thought sets out in detail the form of its own constituent moments, and in so doing establishes the structures of traditional logic. By articulating that subjective structure, thought has given to its own content a fully appropriate form and has thus become fully self-contained. So it not only thinks the concept of objectivity. It has itself become something objective—immediately in and of itself.

Chapter 14

Objectivity

In Hegel's analysis, the disjunctive syllogism, by fully articulating its constituent conditions, is complete in and of itself. That result, removed by understanding from the mediating process that has led up to it, can be called "objectivity." While Hegel admits that this term is frequently used as a synonym for "actuality," "reality" and even "existence," we can, for precision, restrict its sense to that which, in contrast to the self-determining dynamic of conceiving, is unmediated and self-contained. In this sense it is used not only for the world beyond thought, but also for intellectual material, such as the categorical imperative, Plato's ideas, or Kant's causal necessity, which are all thought of as fully self-contained. This concept serves, then, as a dialectical complement for the subjective dynamic of conceiving.

There is, however, something confusing about Hegel's talk of objectivity at this point. For he has already distinguished the third book on the Doctrine of the Concept from the earlier two books by calling the Doctrine of Being and the Doctrine of Essence together "The Objective Logic" and this the "Subjective Logic." How can he then, within the latter, distinguish objectivity from subjectivity?

The categories found in the discussions of being and essence are those we use to think about objects, as distinct from the categories organizing the act of thinking itself. They cover such things as quality and quantity, finitude and measuring, existence and appearance, actuality and substance. Only when we found a category describing objects that matched the ways our own thinking functioned, did we begin to look at the thinking process itself: conceiving, judging and inferring. That triggered the move from the objective logic to the subjective logic.

But why should the subjectivity of conceiving lead us back to objectivity? In the first place, we are now not thinking about those concepts with which we can categorize objects, but about those thoughts whereby we comprehend objectivity as such. To be sure, as we came to the end of the objective logic, concepts like "absolute," "actuality" and "necessity" suggested that we wanted to be comprehensive, incorporating the total picture into our understanding. But we had not achieved a full overview. For that we needed to comprehend the way we think, so that we can then see how thinking grasps objectivity as such. We conceptually organize the whole realm of objects in mechanical, chemical or teleological ways. That is not simply a function of the particular objects being considered, but of the way we think about objects. In other words, we are now explicitly including the activity of thinking in the process of describing objectivity.

In the second place, pure thinking never is content to remain with itself. It is sufficiently comprehensive to recognize its own limits, and in so doing think of what is other than itself. The partiality of subjective reasoning wants to reach the objectivity of secure conclusions so that its own relativity is transcended. This capacity of thought underlies the powerful creativity of the human spirit: it thinks beyond its limits to that which is initially alien. This alone enables it to be truly comprehensive. And once it does so, it no longer thinks about objects as individual units, but about the realm of otherness as a whole. It is objectivity—the realm of what is immediately in and of itself—that is other than subjectivity—the realm of mediation and interconnection.

Mechanism

To conceive of something as immediately in and of itself is to think of a mechanical object.[1] As immediate it is indeterminate; but to be in and of itself, it must be a totality, incorporating all its determinations. Mechanical objectivity, then, involves a universe of objects, each one immediate and indeterminate on its own, but together incorporating all determinations. To resolve the contradiction involved in thinking *indeterminate* objects that yet constitute a *determinate* totality, thought must introduce a process, or becoming, by which each object acts on, and reacts to, the others without thereby losing its distinctive immediacy. This means, however, that this object is no longer completely indeterminate, but its immediate objectivity is the result of an interaction with other objects.

Understood in this way, mechanical objects are no longer indifferent to each other; they particularize themselves in terms of their relationships to each other. The stronger exert an influence over the weaker without thereby destroying their immediate objectivity. They become centres to which the weaker objects respond according to regular patterns or laws. These laws then determine how the independent objects relate to each other.

---

1. Not only physical things can be conceived mechanically. Hobbes constructs his social theory using mechanical categories, with humans functioning as self-contained irreducible units; association psychology uses mechanical concepts to explain the process of thinking, and arithmetic uses mechanical operations to add and subtract.

Conceptual thought thinks of this pattern as a unity, and the result is the thought of objects which are independent, yet oriented towards each other. This is a new kind of objectivity, no longer strictly mechanical, but chemical.

Chemism

With the chemical object as well we have an implicit contradiction— between the independence of the objects, and their mutual orientation. This paradox can be resolved only by positing a process in which their independence is overcome and they become one. Any such process cannot be immediate or direct, else there would be no initial independence. So one must postulate the presence of some kind of mediating object, or catalyst, that, once introduced, will bring about the union.

The product of any such combination can be thought of as a chemical object, however, only if it is not self-contained and inert but, through some other catalyst, can be broken up into independent constituents or elements. And these elements can be considered chemical objects only if they have characteristics that, in appropriate circumstances, enable objects to be chemically oriented towards each other: one as an animating principle, the other as susceptible to animation.

When conceptual thought brings this cycle of processes—chemical union, chemical separation, and the distinctive functions of the elements— together into a unity it realizes that the whole dynamic has a peculiar structure. The processes do not take place immediately, but require media- tion; and that mediation or catalyst does not just happen, but is introduced by conceptual thought to satisfy the original requirements of the concept: chemical object. By taking this whole structure on its own, divorced from the reasoning that led up to it, we have a new category: a framework in which a concept governs or determines which objective processes to use. This is the concept of teleology—of objects being manipulated or orga- nized according to a purpose or goal.

Teleology

When thinking of teleology, or final causes, one distinguishes between a subjective purpose and the objective world in which it is to be realized. Since the objective world is not immediately what it is supposed to become, the subjective purpose must find something immediately at hand that it can use to trigger some objective processes—either mechanical or chemical—that will lead to the desired result. The use of these means bridges the gap between initial purpose and realized end; but they do so not on their own. It is only because they satisfy the requirements of the original purpose that they are useful. In other words a single content persists throughout the whole process. At first it is a concept, pure and simple; then it becomes the governing principle that manipulates instruments and means; in the end it is objectively realized.

While this common content integrates the moments of a teleological process into a single pattern, it nonetheless leads to a paradoxical conclusion. For the objective world is not static. Each end achieved is itself transient, turning into something else; and this means that each particular teleological sequence can be understood as simply a means towards some further end, requiring a larger conceptual framework.[2] We are thus led into an infinite regress in which each end becomes in its turn a means towards a further end.

As we have already seen, conceiving is not impotent before such ongoing repetitions; it can unify syntheses. And so thought looks at this cycle which moves from intention through means to an objective end as a whole, and divorces it from the reasoning that led up to it. What we are now thinking is a whole that is not only objective but also fundamentally determined by the dynamic of subjective conceiving. This kind of objectivity is permeated with subjectivity. Such a relationship between objectivity and subjectivity serves as a primitive definition of life.

With this move we have moved beyond the simple sphere of objectivity. For a full understanding of objects has led to a recognition that subjectivity is important. This development mirrors, in an inverted fashion, the way the subjectivity of conceiving only reaches complete satisfaction when it constructs a disjunctive syllogism, which gives thought an appropriate objective form. We have, then, two transitions: from subjectivity to objectivity and from objectivity to subjectivity. Once again reciprocal interaction sets the stage for a new concept, one which Hegel calls "the Idea." In contrast to concepts, which are primarily subjective, Ideas identify the way subjectivity and objectivity are to be united—that is to say, those contexts where concepts are realized. For thought has the plastic ability not only to think beyond its limits, but also to think of ways by which it can be interconnected with whatever is radically distinct from its own conceiving.

---

2. This, Hegel will suggest elsewhere, is the rational underpinning for the teleological arguments for the existence of God.

Chapter 15

The Idea

Life

With the category of "life" thought is thinking of subjectivity and objectivity as integrated into a unity. Just as the analysis of conceiving led to what is immediately in and of itself (and so objective), so the analysis of immediate objectivity has led to an objectivity permeated by conceptual subjectivity. Each reflects the other in a single perspective. The categories which integrate this synthesis of subjectivity and objectivity into one thought are more than simple concepts, however; for they incorporate that which is other than mere conceiving, or objectivity. To name this distinctive kind of thought, Hegel adopts from the tradition the word: idea. For Plato an idea or form was objective, in the sense that it is immediately in and of itself, yet is just as much a subjective conceiving. This is the sense Hegel prefers, rather than the one advanced by Kant. For his ideas do not simply regulate the function of reason as Kant's do; they also capture the truth of objectivity.

The category "idea," however, will also undergo revision as we render its definition more precise. It starts out as the simple identity of the subjective and the objective—what we have adopted as the most elementary definition of "life." But this is no indeterminate identity; for we have come to it through the discussion of teleology where the subjective concept organizes objectivity. Where the two are completely integrated, as they now are, the various components are no longer independent mechanical objects, but have become members of a single body—a living individual. Governed by the subjective "soul," these members interact, each one both determining, and determined by, the others. They do this by being open, or sensitive, to each other; by reacting to the others in a process the contemporary biologists called irritability; and by integrating both openness and resistance and thereby reconstituting their own unique functioning—what was then called reproduction.

Since this structure of mutual interaction characterizes life, it must apply not only to this reciprocal dynamic where members of a single body interact with each other, but also to the way that integrated individual interacts with its environment. As sensitive, the individual is open to, and able to overreach, this alien other, even though this latter has its own agenda. At the same time the living individual resists the intrusions of that environment when its own integrity is threatened. And it combines both moments by appropriating that other and transforming its independent prickliness into a component of its own life. In this way it renews itself as an individual—no longer strictly identical with what it was before, but similar enough to be the same kind of thing, or genus.[1]

With the thought of "genus" we are thinking of a structure of life common to several individuals. But these individuals need not be reconstituted versions of a single living process over time, different simply because different objective elements have been appropriated in different circumstances. They could equally well be independent individuals that share a common structure. As something simply shared, however, the genus is in danger of becoming nothing but an abstract universal, not a living union of objectivity with subjectivity. For all that it has emerged as a concept or category, it does not have any objective existence of its own; it is not yet an idea. Since it is supposed to be the universal expression of life, however, the genus should integrate actuality with thought, objectivity with subjectivity. This union can be achieved when what is common (and so generic) to two individuals becomes objective as a seed. This achievement, however, is flawed; for when the seed develops it becomes just another individual instance of the genus. The genus thus remains abstract, even though it continues to provide the impetus for another union of two individuals in a new seed—a cycle that continues in an infinite progression.

Once again Hegel uses an infinite progression (or regression) as the launching pad for a new concept. For once thought conceives this recurring cycle as a unity, it realizes that something has been achieved. For the genus has found its corresponding objectivity—not in any single seed or living individual, but rather in the ongoing cycle of reproduction. What we have is not a simple identity of subjective genus and objective cycle that mimics the integrity of a living individual, but rather a correspondence between a conceptual universal, or genus, and an objective reality where it is continually instantiated. If we focus on that feature of correspondence between two universals, one subjective and the other objective, and leave aside the reasoning that led to it, we have a new category: the correspondence of subjectivity with objectivity, which frequently serves as the definition of what we call "cognition" or "knowledge."

---

1. "Genus" as it first emerges, then, refers not to that which a number of distinct individuals share, but to the various incarnations of the same individual as it is modified and transformed through its interaction with its environment.

Cognition

In cognition conceptual thought first distinguishes itself from its object, which now stands over against it as a distinctive other. At the same time it has the drive to establish a correspondence with that other—to capture its form conceptually. This defines the cognitive quest: to establish under the "idea of the true" a correspondence between object and concept. This quest progresses through several stages.

Conceptual thought starts by trying to grasp the object as it is, without introducing any mediating activity of its own. Since there are to be no conceptual discriminations, the object is thought in the form of a simple identity—as an abstract universal. Not only is the object as such conceived in this way, but each concrete characteristic by which it is distinguished from other objects is identified as an independent universal on its own.

Thought thereby *analyses* an object into its elements—a collection of diverse universals—which, though originating from the same object, yet have no conceptual relationship one to another. Any such synthesis, after all, would require that mediating activity of thought which we have tried to hold in check to ensure complete objectivity. Were thought to consider instead the whole object as distinct from its parts, or as a cause that has certain effects, any correspondence would be lost, unless these connections are not the product of reflective thought, but rather relationships found within the object itself. This would presuppose, however, that the object itself is not simply a collection of analysed components, but a universal that determines itself into particulars, a force that effects its own expression. Thought would then not be constructing these kinds of relationships but simply mirroring them in its own activity. To achieve a full correspondence between concept and object, then, the concept must try to reproduce the object's synthetic dynamic, and so mimic objective mediation in its own cognitive endeavour.

The first synthetic move the concept makes is to construct a definition of the object. Even though the latter is considered to be a singular, thought subsumes it under a universal genus, and then distinguishes it by means of its specific differences. While this process can be quite successful when the object is already the work of abstract reason (as in mathematics), it becomes much less effective when thought tries to establish the defining characteristics of real objects in the natural and social world. For something that specifically differentiates humans—the lobe of the ear, for example—does not necessarily capture anything very essential about them. And the wider genus could be defined by any common features whatever, whether essential or not.[2] In addition, malformed individuals are

---

2. For example, although the extinct Tasmanian thylacine filled the biological space for wolves in that environment, and has been classified as such, it is a marsupial rather than a mammal.

born into any species, requiring exceptions. So the work of definition on its own is prone to error and cannot provide the desired correspondence.

The strategy adopted to avoid this difficulty is the method of division. Whereas definition starts from the singular object and tries to derive both its universal genus and its specific difference, division starts from a universal and then distinguishes within this universal its particular species. Any such division should be exhaustive, capturing all the various components of the universal. While this move, like the preceding one, can be successful when used with the abstract objects of conceptual systems, it is nonetheless woefully inept when applied to concrete objects in nature and society. For the universal by itself lacks any principle that determines how it is to be broken up into particulars, since it expresses only what is common to a number of objects.

Thought tries to resolve this dilemma by constructing theorems that articulate the rationale by which the universal and its components are mutually related to each other. While at this point Hegel spends his time talking about the theorems of Euclid (which illustrate only conceptual systems), the approach he defines could equally apply to the formulation of hypotheses and theories in natural science, in which thought articulates a network of internal relations to explain how a whole is articulated into its parts or a set of conditions combines to produce a determinate effect.

This type of cognition shows how the various elements of the object may be related to each other; nonetheless it fails in its turn to attain full correspondence. For it remains the subjective act of conceiving that constructs this network of interrelations, and there is no guarantee that the object itself is in fact determined and formed in this way. A carefully constructed hypothesis, even if it explains all the known facts, need not be true.[3]

This means that a completely new approach must be taken to achieve the desired correspondence. Instead of working with the "idea of the true," thought starts from the "idea of the good"—a conceptual structure that interconnects determinate moments and then wills to realize this thought objectively. By making the world fit our concepts we hope to reach our goal of a full correspondence between concept and actuality.

These hopes also remain unrealized, however, because the objective world has its own structure and its own agenda, and the practical idea (or will) finds itself confronted by unconquerable limits which frustrate its

---

3. The difficulties that have emerged in the various strategies of cognition are not the result of failed attempts at practical application. They rather stem from thought recognizing the limits of its own procedures. Indeed, even in scientific practice, there is a difference between maintaining the theory and trying to fit the facts to it, and recognizing in advance that the theory itself cannot cover all expected eventualities. Taking account of that difference is itself the result of thinking, not of observation.

intentions. To the extent that the idea of the good—with its aim of realizing its conceptual construction in reality on its own—is separated from cognition, or the idea of the true, it will be as unsuccessful as the latter when *it* is divorced from willed action. Each, then, requires the other if there is to be any hope of achieving a full correspondence between concept and object—of realizing what Hegel has called the idea.

The Absolute Idea

In other words, the idea in and of itself involves integrating the theoretical drive for truth with the practical drive to achieve the good. Not only does each complement the other, but each on its own shows up the limitations of the other. The characteristics of the object identified by analysis show to practical reason the determinations which it must build into its idea of the good; and the success or failure of the attempts to realize the good confirms or belies the theoretical constructions of pure cognition.

With this we have a reciprocal relationship which is complete in itself, and can be collapsed into a new unified concept to which Hegel gives the name "absolute idea." When theory and practice continually check and reinforce each other we have a way of integrating concept and actuality that is valid in all respects.[4] The final task of Hegel's *Logic* is to explore what happens when this dynamic is integrated into a single thought. It involves the method common to both theory and practice and so underpinning the whole proceeding discussion.

The method of pure reason starts from something immediate. The fact that it is the beginning means that no mediation that might have led to it is being considered. As immediate it is simple and universal. Though universal, however, this beginning has a particular character—it is in itself some distinctive thing. The task of thought is to take this beginning and articulate its specific determination.

Any such determination, once isolated, is inevitably different from the original simplicity. So thought moves on to the moment of difference: of determination over against indeterminacy, of defining limit over against inherent nature. Yet when it focuses on this new moment of difference, thought finds that it is led back to *its* opposite, which is the concept with which we began. On the one hand these two reciprocal processes are the way we analyze what is already there; on the other hand we are introducing synthetically new material because unity has been dissolved into difference. This, says Hegel, is the moment of dialectic.

---

4. As we have seen, this definition of "absolute" as "valid in all respects" is derived from Kant's *Critique of Pure Reason* B381, Kemp Smith, p. 317.

Working out the differences that have emerged in detail leads from an initial diversity into opposition and—when each moment is recognized as fully defining the original beginning—contradiction. Since these contradictory moments developed from a continuous process of thought, they are related not simply negatively as opposites, but each is also the result of the other; each is required because it is conditioned by the other.

When, using speculative reason, we look at this relationship as a whole, we have reciprocal interaction which is both positive and negative—each rejects the other, yet each presupposes and requires the other. We need, then, to work out how the various moments can be incorporated into a more comprehensive perspective while cancelling their independence.

Both the immediate dialectical inference that leads to an opposing, distinctive term and the reflective speculative synthesis which considers the opposites in both their negative and positive relationship are moves familiar in ordinary discussions of reasoning. What is distinctively Hegelian is the final move, in which the speculative synthesis is then united into a single concept, complete in itself, which can be considered on its own apart from all the mediation that led up to it. We have already seen that Kant called this the work of understanding—generating concepts as discursive functions of unity. As Hegel has shown in his discussion of concepts,[5] such conceiving involves particularizing a thought until one has identified it as a singular. As a unity it is universal incorporating a number of elements; as now given a new immediacy through abstraction, however, it is indeterminate in form, even though its content includes the results of the earlier development. Conceiving thus introduces a new beginning ready for further dialectical analysis. This move by understanding, Hegel says, is the third, after dialectical and speculative reason; but he admits it could also be called the fourth: beginning, transition to another and back to the first, synthesis, new beginning.

It is this final move, where conceptual thought creates a new immediate beginning out of a complex development, that enables Hegel to set his discussion of the movement of thought into a system. Each stage develops through complications towards a new beginning. And when we reach a conclusion that includes all conceptual determinations whatever—the absolute idea—we collapse this complex into a new single thought which, having nothing other that it can be distinguished from, can only be indeterminate. We have returned to the concept of simple self-equivalence, which is nothing else but the "being" with which we began. The *Logic* has come full circle.

---

5. In Chapter 12.

At times in logical thought the various moments of the method fall apart. The dialectical moment leads to ever more detailed analysis without synthesis. The speculative moment ascends to ever more encompassing, and abstract, universals. Only when the two contrary moments are integrated, however, can rational thought hope to be fully comprehensive.[6]

With this Hegel has competed his *Logic*. The discussion of method captures the full nature of thought that thinks only its pure concepts, for it describes the dynamic that is common both to the subjectivity of the concept and the objectivity of whatever is conceived. For all that continued analysis and reflection may reveal new details that need to be incorporated into the logical discussion, its method, and so its distinctive essence, is fully transparent.[7]

Yet Hegel has not finished his philosophy. For thought is always able to think beyond its limits. When considering the realm of transparent interconnections which characterizes pure thought it can wonder what it would be like to have a different realm, where the opposite holds sway—where everything simply is what it is, externally related to everything else. Thought, with its passion for comprehension, cannot anticipate what that realm, radically different from itself, would in fact be like. But we can recognize that it is possible, and that we can discover what it is like, not by trying to think it out on its own, but by abandoning our passion for comprehensive control and being open to whatever comes.

Pure thought can, indeed, expect more. For in the course of its own development it has come upon concepts which articulate elements of difference: "other," "difference," "external," "contingent," "particular," and so on. And it has learned that every time it came upon such terms, implicit connections led to more comprehensive perspectives. So philosophical thought anticipates that it already has some concepts that can do justice to the external world it discovers, and that, by integrating those prior concepts with whatever determinate characteristics the given shows itself to have, we can develop more comprehensive concepts which may, in their turn,

---

6. It is worth noting that this final achievement of the absolute idea, while valid in all respects, does not necessarily reach closure. For the result of the method is to reach a new immediate which, as immediate, simply provides a new beginning. Similarly, the reciprocal interaction of theoretical and practical reason enables each to correct and modify the other, but since each functions on its own, neither can fully resolve the incompleteness of the other. Each can, so to speak, show up the inadequacies of the other, but never fully confirm or realize what the other proposes, either as the true or the good. Paradoxically, Hegel could be espousing a fallibilism that anticipates both Pierce and Popper.

7. "I could not pretend," writes Hegel, "that the method which I follow in this system of Logic—or rather which this system in its own self follows—is not capable of greater completeness, of much elaboration in detail; but at the same time I know that it is the only true method." *SL* 54; *GW* 21: 38.

find instantiation in the real world. So we can turn to this alien realm of otherness, confident that it is not impervious to thought but can be understood and comprehended. To that realm we give the name "nature."

Hegel has, then, provided the entrée to the rest of his system. The end of the *Logic* does not just lead back to its own beginning. It also opens the door to a new beginning, in which philosophy explains and understands the world of nature and human society which lies outside the purview of pure thought.

PART V

The *Encyclopaedia Logic*

Chapter 16

The *Encyclopaedia Logic* and the *Science of Logic*

That Hegel did not hold the *Science of Logic* to be complete in every detail can be seen in what he himself did with it. The original three-volume work was written while he was still headmaster of the classical secondary school in Nürnberg, before he finally acquired tenured positions, first at Heidelberg and then at Berlin. Once he got to Heidelberg, he needed a textbook for his courses which would be more manageable than the highly theoretical volumes of the *Phenomenology of Spirit* or the *Logic*. So he wrote an *Encyclopaedia of the Philosophical Sciences in Outline* "for use in his lectures."[1] It includes not only a version of the *Science of Logic*, but also a Philosophy of Nature and a Philosophy of Spirit.

The *Encyclopaedia* is made up of a series of compact paragraphs. They provide a skeleton that is to be fleshed out in Hegel's oral presentation. When we compare its first part, which encapsulates the *Science of Logic*, with that earlier work we find that (in the first edition) it contained 181 paragraphs covering 112 pages, to cover the material that took three decent sized volumes in the Nürnberg work. The second edition expanded this to 226 paragraphs and 188 pages.[2] This page count includes the remarks Hegel added (as he had done earlier) to show how the abstract philosophical kernel of the basic paragraphs could be applied to the history of philosophy, to current debates, or to contemporary work in other disciplines. Wallace's English translation sets these remarks in the same typeface as the basic

---

1. This phrase is found on the title page of all three editions. Consider also the opening of his preface to the first edition: "The need to give into the hands of my audience a guiding thread for my philosophical lectures is the immediate inducement for allowing this overview of the whole extent of philosophy to see the light earlier than my intentions had been." *GW* 13: 5; compare p. 1 of *The Encyclopaedia Logic*, tr. Geraets, Suchting and Harris (Indianapolis: Hackett, 1991).
2. In this count I have not included the preliminary material, for which there is no counterpart in the larger work. I have taken the page count from the critical edition (*GW*). The comparable page count for the 1812–1816 *Science of Logic* would be 623.

paragraph, and so fails to discriminate between what is essential, and what (for Hegel) is commentary. Fortunately the translation prepared by Geraets, Suchting and Harris does recognize the difference.

The *Encyclopaedia* as a whole received an extensive revision ten years later, growing from 477 to 574 paragraphs. Further amendments as well as three paragraphs originally in the 1816 version were added in 1830. Then, after Hegel's death in 1831, this outline became the foundation for what his disciples called his "System of Philosophy." Realizing that flesh had to be added to the skeleton, they assembled lecture notes taken by students over the years as well as manuscripts Hegel himself had used when lecturing, some from as far back as 1803. From these they prepared what have been called "additions"—further comments which report how Hegel had, on one occasion or another, expanded on the printed paragraph. By collating many different lecture sequences, some from before the *Science of Logic* itself took definite shape, they ignored the way Hegel modified the flow and sequence of his discussion from year to year.[3] At the same time, however, they provided a text that is more accessible to the average philosophical reader than either the original *Science of Logic* or the dense telegraphic theses that make up each primary paragraph of the *Encyclopaedia*.

Only in the last few decades has there been a renewed interest in the way Hegel developed his thoughts in a single lecture course; and how he changed his presentation from year to year. We now have available two sets of lecture notes from his course on the Logic: one from Heidelberg in 1817, when the *Encyclopaedia* was hot off the press, the other (taken by Hegel's son, Karl) from his final series in the summer of 1831. This means that we can begin to see how Hegel moved orally from concept to concept for a single class of students.

In writing the *Encyclopaedia Logic*, Hegel was not simply expecting to expand the summary theses into a full-fledged oral presentation. He also knew that his audience had access to the fuller version already published. So he was content to produce what could be called merely an "outline." "The nature of an outline excludes not only an exhaustive development of the ideas in terms of their content, but restricts in particular the development of their systematic derivation, a derivation that must contain what one usually understands under 'proof,' and that is inescapable for a scientific philosophy."[4]

So it is worth looking at the differences between the larger *Science of Logic* and the shorter *Encyclopaedia Logic*.

---

3. In Berlin, for example, Hegel lectured on the *Logic* during the summer semester every year from 1819 to 1831.

4. Preface to the First Edition, second paragraph. *GW* 13: 5; *The Encyclopaedia Logic*, 1. He goes on to express regret that he has not been able to provide the same detailed argument for the philosophies of nature and spirit as he already had done for his logic.

The dense prose of the earlier work uses the abstract language of conceptual thought to indicate the moves reason makes as it reflects on concepts. The text has little illustrative content, for Hegel assumes that the reader will grasp the pure conceptual meaning, as well as those implications that connect it to preceding and subsequent terms. Even so, the moves he makes are detailed and painstakingly articulated. He offers a rarefied and sophisticated discourse that few navigate with ease. At times he may interrupt this strictly logical development with remarks that apply what he has written to mathematics, the history of philosophy, contemporary science, or theology, but these offer little help in grasping the systematic argument of his basic thought, although they do suggest what he has in mind at each stage.

In the *Encyclopaedia* an analysis and development that might take several pages in the longer work is telegraphed into a single paragraph of two or three sentences. If we consider simply the discussion of "measure" (even Hegel admits that it is one of the most difficult sections), the only kind of measuring mentioned is the use of a rule, after which he moves directly to the "measureless" and the reciprocal relation between the measureless and measure.[5] Similar abbreviations, though not always so drastic, are found throughout. He tends to expand his discussions, using several paragraphs, only when he makes one of his characteristic transitions—where a reciprocal interaction collapses into a new concept.

Because the English text of the *Encyclopaedia Logic* is largely made up of the illustrative material found in Hegel's remarks and the editorial additions from his lectures, it has become the most accessible introduction to Hegel's *Logic*. It certainly indicates the overall framework, and gives ample evidence of how he saw his logic being applied to mathematics, science, philosophy and religion. What it lacks is the careful tracing of the argument as a concept shifts into its antithesis; as that shift elaborates into several versions of the same concept, each more intricate in meaning; as the contrary meanings turn out to imply and presuppose each other; and as this mutual interaction provides a comprehensive new way of thinking our terms. Not able to take the space for such an elaborate development, Hegel, in the *Encyclopaedia Logic*, draws parallels between each new stage and comparable moves made earlier; the reader has to remember that, for all the similarity, we are working with new conceptual content, requiring new meanings.

The *Encyclopaedia* includes more than a summary of the earlier *Science of Logic*. By the time Hegel came to the second edition in 1827, he realized that he could not rely on the summary introduction of 1816, and he needed to show how and why he approached philosophy as he did. Rather than retracing the long tortuous path of the *Phenomenology of Spirit*, he shows

---

5. That he did not intend this to be a permanent reduction can be seen in the detailed revision of the longer discussion in the second edition of the *Science of Logic* in 1831. Compare Chapter 8.

how his thought relates to the standard philosophical positions of his day: traditional metaphysics, empiricism, the Kantian philosophy, and the return to immediate intuition, characteristic of the romantics generally, but developed most clearly in the thought of Friedrich Jacobi. This "Preliminary Concept" is added to the beginning of the section on the Logic.

From the Logic, as well, Hegel moved on to the other parts of his philosophical system: the philosophies of nature and of spirit. The former takes up the natural sciences: mechanics, physics, chemistry, geology and biology. The latter discusses the human sciences, both those concerned with the individual (like psychology) and those concerned with society (like politics and economics). The *Encyclopaedia* concludes with a discussion of those spheres of human activity where we try to capture the complete picture: art, religion and philosophy.

Originally Hegel had intended to write full treatises on these latter two sections—treatises that would carry on the tradition of the larger *Science of Logic*. Once he became involved in the treadmill of regular lecture courses, two each semester, which covered all of these areas as well as the philosophy of history, and which required constant updating with respect to the most recent discoveries in science, the most recent reports from world travellers, the most recent developments in politics, particularly in western Europe, this program fell away. He did expand the section on politics and economics, originally called "Objective Spirit," into the *Philosophy of Right*. And he declared his intention to do the same for his Anthropology, Phenomenology and Psychology. But these works were to follow the same pattern as the *Encyclopaedia*. Rather than a prose discourse, developing an ongoing, flowing argument, the *Philosophy of Right* is a series of paragraphs with remarks (and later additions), to be used in his lectures. Once again we have a number of discrete units that do not represent the way thought moves from concept to concept.

The *Encyclopaedia*, with its three editions, raises several questions that merit further discussion. In the first place, when we compare the three different versions with the original *Science of Logic* and with the second edition of its first part on the Doctrine of Being (that was published just after Hegel's death), we can see that Hegel made a number of changes over time. What do these alterations tell us about Hegel's project for a science of pure thought? In the second place, the *Encyclopaedia* is meant to be a compendium for Hegel's lectures. How did he expand this material in his oral presentations? By looking at the two sets of notes now readily available we can see how he approached the difficult task of making philosophy accessible to a wider audience. In the third place, how can Hegel make the transition from the science of pure thought to the philosophies of nature and spirit? Schelling called this move an illegitimate shift into another genus. How can it be made while retaining a systematic development? And what role does the logic continue to play, once we start thinking about that which is other than thought, nature both physical and human? And finally, what role does the logic play in structuring the important lecture courses devoted to the four realms where we consider the world comprehensively: history, art, religion and philosophy? In all of these Hegel claims to be presenting his material scientifically, and not just following a contingent, subjective ordering. What does he mean by this claim?

To a consideration of these questions in sequence we now turn.

Chapter 17

How Hegel Changed His Mind

From the time, just after Hegel's death in 1831, that his disciples brought out his works in a "Complete Edition by an Association of Friends of the Immortalized," it was widely assumed that Hegel had developed a complete and exhaustive system that covered all the bases. That last word, "immortalized" (*Verewigten* in German), suggested that here was a fully worked out philosophy that would stand the test of time.[1] For true believers, this meant that one could find in Hegel's writing an answer to all significant questions; for the more sceptical it was evidence of his presumptuous pride.

About a century later, in 1905, Wilhelm Dilthey published an account of Hegel's early years, based on manuscripts from his years in Tübingen, Bern and Frankfurt, which showed that he had started with quite different views of religion, politics and philosophic method from the positions found in his later lectures.[2] About the same time, Georg Lasson brought out editions of manuscripts from Hegel's years in Jena, when he was starting to work out a more systematic perspective. From this evidence it became clear that the Hegelian system had not sprung complete from his head, like Minerva from the head of Jupiter.

Since then we have become more aware of how Hegel modified and developed his system over time. An edition that reprinted much of the friends' edition of 1845 in the early twentieth century included

---

1. When the editors gave as much weight to material from the lectures of 1803 as to that from 1831 they implied that "the system" was static and complete, right from the beginning.
2. W. Dilthey, *Die Jugendgeschichte Hegels*, Berlin: Reimer, 1905. While this was translated into Japanese in 1929, it has never appeared in English. A student of Dilthey, Hermann Nohl, published a selection of Hegel's early essays, *Hegels Theologische Jugendschriften*, in 1907 (Tübingen: Mohr); some of these were translated by T.M. Knox and Richard Kroner in G.W.F. Hegel, *Early Theological Writings* (Chicago: University of Chicago Press, 1948).

the 1816 Heidelberg *Encyclopaedia*[3] in addition to the later system; the first edition of the Doctrine of Being from the *Science of Logic*, now available in German,[4] makes evident how many changes Hegel introduced in the "standard" second edition (which has simply been included with the first edition of the other two parts by his editors); a critical edition of lecture notes from his course on the philosophy of religion has shown how radically Hegel had changed the organization of the course over the four times he presented it.[5] As a result we are now much more aware that Hegel's philosophy was a system in progress, constantly being revised and rethought. The idea of an immortalized monolith has been shattered.

The *Logic* has been the last to be subjected to this new perspective. One could understand that, as Hegel learned the results of the latest science, as he read the most recent reports of travellers to distant places, as new political developments emerged, he would amend and adjust what he had to say about nature, politics, history, religion and art. But thought is more permanent. Once one has articulated the system of pure reason, thinking has a reliability and objectivity that ensures our reaching true conclusions from true premises whenever and wherever we follow its precepts.

In fact, however, we find that Hegel was ready to modify and adjust his logical material quite extensively. In some cases we can identify five different written stages. There is the full first edition of the large *Science of Logic*; there are the three editions of the *Encyclopaedia Logic* (though the third edition made few substantive changes to the second); and there is the second edition of the first book on the Doctrine of Being.

Some examples may illustrate the kind of changes he made. In the first edition of the *Science of Logic*, the basic discussion of *Dasein* follows this order of categories: "*Dasein*," "being other," "being for another" and "being in itself," "reality," and then "something." Hegel then proceeded from "limit" through "determination," "quality," "alteration" and "negation" to "infinity." By the second edition of 1831 the shift from "*Dasein*" to "something" moves quite directly by way of "quality." Then Hegel moves from "something" to "other," "being in itself" and "for another," "determination," "limit" and "finitude" before reaching a much expanded discussion of "qualitative infinity." The earlier categories of "reality" and "negation" (which he had taken over from Kant) are reduced to elements within the discussion of "quality."

---

3. This can now be found in an English translation: G.W.F. Hegel, *Encyclopedia of the Philosophical Sciences in Outline and Critical Writings*, ed. E. Behler, The German Library, Vol 24 (New York: Continuum, 1990).

4. *GW* 11; P.J. Labarrière and G. Jarczyk translated the first edition into French in *Science de la Logique* (Paris: Aubier, 1972).

5. G.W.F. Hegel, *Lectures on the Philosophy of Religion*, tr. by R.F. Brown, P.C. Hodgson and J.M. Stewart (Berkeley: University of California Press, 1984, 1985 & 1987), a translation of *V* 3, 4a, 4b, and 5.

When one turns to the three editions of the *Encyclopaedia* (which span the whole interim period between the two versions of the larger work) we find that Hegel changed the order of the categories several times. Already in 1817, "quality" introduces the discussion of "being other," "being for other," "being in itself," "reality" and "something," rather than appearing later. By 1827 "quality" alone remains in this first set of moves, anticipating Hegel's last position, but "negation" and "reality" continue to play a role in the transition from "something" to "limitation" and "finitude."

Some new material added in the 1831 second edition of the larger *Logic* suggests that, in the time since 1812, Hegel had become aware of the need to differentiate the simple transitions of being, when one term simply passes over into its successor, from the work of reflection, which simultaneously thinks contraries as directly referring to each other. In other words he has become more careful in distinguishing the way the different operations of thought—immediate transitions, reflective syntheses, and conceptual unities—function so that they are not introduced prematurely nor become caught up in a confusing mélange.

A second example of Hegel's reworking of material is his discussion of the German term, *Sache*. This word, difficult to translate, is conventionally used for a number of purposes: a legal case, a task, a question under discussion, the business at hand, the subject or theme. Earlier in this exposition I used "nature of things," when it emerged within the discussion of "ground" in its transition to the concept of "existence."[6] That exposition reflected the text of 1813.

That particular text, as part of the Doctrine of Essence, never was revised. However, *Sache* disappeared completely from the 1817 version of the *Encyclopaedia* to re-emerge in 1827 in the discussion of "real possibility." Though this appears much later in the Doctrine of Essence—in the material on the modal categories rather than as a final stage in the discussion of "ground"—it nonetheless retains associations with the 1813 text. For in the digested version of the *Logic* for his students, Hegel discusses the structure of conditioning only at this point—a set of conditions constitutes a real possibility—rather than earlier as the way a complete ground functions. To this extent there remains some parallelism to the 1813 text.

The most significant change, however, occurs in 1831. For Hegel now introduces *Sache* into the final stages of his discussion of measure, toward the end of his first book on the Doctrine of Being.[7] He uses it to name the reality that underlies the surface change of qualities whenever quantitative ratios are varied. In this discussion it anticipates the distinction between an essence and its superficial show, rather than being one part of the logic developed from that distinction. It would seem that, in reworking the way

---

6. See Chapter 9.
7. Recall that the *Encyclopaedia* truncated the discussion of "measuring" severely.

changes of quantitive ratios produce qualitative shifts even though the underling components remain the same, Hegel has discovered that he is preparing the way for a primitive sense of "substratum" for which "substance" would be too specific, and "essence" would pre-empt the shift to the second part of the *Logic*. So he draws on *Sache* to satisfy his needs. Because the second book was never revised, we shall never know what he intended to do once he got to the discussion of conditioning, ground and existence.

We can, however, see him reworking the Doctrine of Essence quite extensively as he expanded his *Encyclopaedia*. By 1830 he no longer starts this book with a substantive discussion of the various forms of reflection. Instead, he moves directly to the "determinations of reflection": identity, difference and ground. "Existence" and "thing" are now included in the first part, which has been renamed "essence as ground of existence"; the second part, on "appearance" includes the distinction between content and form, earlier found in "ground"; the third part, "actuality" omits any reference to "the absolute," and includes the three moments of "condition," "the thing itself" (*Sache*), and "activity," all found originally in "ground."

A further change is also of interest. In the 1816 Doctrine of the Concept, the "singular" is the end point of the process of conceptual determination, when it reaches something that is defined so much by negation that it cannot be thought as a concept but only indicated. This sense continues in the first edition of the *Encyclopaedia* a year later. In 1827 Hegel adds a qualification to his Remark on Paragraph 163:[8] "Singularity is not to be taken in the sense of *immediate* singularity, as when we speak of singular things or men; these determinations of singularity emerge only in judgement." But he makes a significant further addition three years later: "Each moment of the concept is itself the whole concept (§ 160), but the singularity, the subject is the concept *posited* as totality." In other words, the singular is the way we think any conceptual structure *as a whole*. That sense has not been brought out as explicitly before.

These examples show that Hegel was constantly rethinking his material: drawing important new distinctions, while allowing earlier ones to recede into the background.

The *Science of Logic*, then, is not a closed study, fully complete on the death of Hegel. Indeed he was revising and reworking the material up to the moment of his death. One could say that the method he described in the final chapter on the absolute idea was continuing to function. Any ordered analysis of the structure of pure thought, once complete, became a new beginning which was then subject to revision and alteration—changes that would have to be reintegrated systematically into a coherent discussion. Whether these alterations are simply efforts by Hegel to correct his earlier

---

8. In the first edition of *EL*, this is §111.

thought on the way to a complete and closed system, or whether the process of revision is endemic to the logical method itself is a question that cannot be decided on the evidence we have.

Although the logic underwent a number of revisions, Hegel nonetheless claimed that the method articulated in the chapter on the absolute idea is the only true method. Because revising involves the move into something other, a reciprocal move back again, the synthesis of the two, and finally the collapse into a new immediate unity, it is not simply one moment in an infinite regress. For the new beginning is, in a sense, simply the earlier starting point now enriched with new determinations and new content. So what from one point of view could be read as a movement on to new determinations could also be seen as an exploration of the presuppositions underlying that indeterminate beginning. And since the pattern is self-correcting, in that the move to difference shows the inadequacies of what had gone on before, it is able to reaffirm its own validity even as it is subject to revision. The method is, therefore, valid in all respects, or absolute.

Chapter 18

Lectures on the Logic

The *Encyclopaedia of the Philosophical Sciences in Outline* was designed as a compendium or handbook that would provide the framework for Hegel's courses, first in Heidelberg, and then in Berlin. Even in his third edition of 1830, Hegel notes that: "Nonetheless for the compendium-like purpose of the text-book, the style must remain constrained as terse, formal and abstract; it receives its determination only by receiving the necessary elaboration through an oral presentation."[1]

When Leopold von Henning undertook to prepare both the larger *Science of Logic* and the *Encyclopaedia Logic* for the first edition of Hegel's works in the 1830s he and his colleagues realized that a definitive edition required that the succinct prose of the printed text be expanded by the more detailed material that Hegel had provided in his lectures. Since Hegel had left behind no manuscript for his oral presentation, von Henning gathered together sets of student notes, from several different lecture sequences.

After giving one course on "Logic and Metaphysics" in Heidelberg in 1817, Hegel began to lecture on this part of his system in his first summer in Berlin, in 1819, and continued to give the course every summer from then until the year of his death in 1831. In other words, there were fourteen different occasions when Hegel worked through this material orally.

Von Henning reports that, for his purposes, he used the notes he himself had written out after each lecture for the courses of 1819 and 1820, as well as the similar manuscripts of Heinrich Hotho (who edited the lectures on the aesthetics) and Karl Michelet (whose assignment was the philosophy of nature and the lectures on the history of philosophy). Although we do not have any definite date for

---

1. First paragraph of the Foreword to the Third Edition. *GW* 20: 27; *The Encyclopaedia Logic*, tr. Geraets, Suchting & Harris (Indianapolis: Hackett, 1991) 18.

these, they likely came from the years around 1823. A fifth set of notes "from a later time," written by "Herr Deputy Principal Geyer," was probably derived from the lectures of 1830.

With notes from five different offerings of the course on "Logic and Metaphysics" (as it was called in the prospectus until the summer of 1831, when it became just "Logic"), von Henning's task was to find the material that was appropriate to each of the 244 paragraphs of the first part of the *Encyclopaedia*. This involved not only cutting and pasting, but trying to make the result as coherent and readable as possible. In the Foreword to his edition he says:

> Although now in this endeavour care was certainly taken throughout to give Hegel's actual expressions and turns of phrase, nonetheless it lay in the nature of things that an external diplomatic exactitude could not be made of first importance in the editorial strategy, but that, above everything, care must be taken to rework the material, distributed among the diverse texts from several lecture sequences, into a coherent whole, so that there may be offered to those who, lacking any other preparation in philosophical thinking, first turn to the study of speculative logic that assistance so desirable in so difficult a study. In following this goal, the editor has not scrupled, in those instances where the material immediately available did not suffice, to complete the elaborations that seemed required from his own memory.[2]

We have then, an edited collation of a number of texts, organized according to the understanding of the editor. The additions von Henning made to the *Encyclopaedia Logic* can only with considerable reservation be attributed directly to Hegel. Not only are they first filtered through the minds of the students who listened to the lectures and then went home to write out a fair copy of what was said, but also through the organizing principles of the final editor.

Something else was lost in the process. For what is important for Hegel is the systematic flow of thought that leads from concept to concept. He is not simply interested in illustrating the compact and dense prose of his compendium, making it accessible to his audience, but also in showing how one thought leads on to the next. For this is what is philosophically significant. In this he was reasonably successful. Ludwig Feuerbach, writing to his father during the summer semester of 1824 reported that: "Hegel in his lectures is not nearly so obtuse as he is in his writing; indeed I could say he is clear and easily understandable. For he takes a great deal of consideration of the stage of the ability to grasp and conceptualize at which most of his audience stand. In other respects—and that is what is so

---

2. All this material is reproduced from the Introduction to Udo Rameil's edition of the Lectures of 1831, *V* 10: XIII-XIX.

magnificent about his lectures—even when he develops the material, the concept, the idea not in itself, not pure and isolated in its elements, he nonetheless always remains firmly with the kernel of the material."[3]

That dynamic and movement by which conceptual thought develops is lost when material is organized under distinct paragraphs, collated with related material from other lectures, and then edited into a kind of footnote to a published text. While the expanded *Encyclopaedia*, with its additions, has made Hegel's logic more accessible to the general reader, then, it has not really provided us with the philosophical process by which thought moves from concept to concept—that process which justifies Hegel's claim to having produced a system.

Now, however, we are beginning to get a picture of how Hegel developed a single series of lectures. To be sure the texts that von Henning used have not been found, and are presumed lost. But recently, in a Swiss library, there was found a clear, well written set of lecture notes written by a law student during Hegel's first lectures on the logic and metaphysics in Heidelberg in 1817. And the notes taken by Hegel's son, Karl, from the final lectures in 1831, have also been published.

The two sets of notes are quite different. In 1817, for all that the first edition of the *Encyclopaedia* had just appeared, Hegel appears to have lectured by dictation. Even though the student, F.A. Good, took down his notes in the course of the lecture, these are clear, well organized, and follow coherently from point to point. At the same time the material discussed is quite dense. Hegel is not as prone, as he was later, to expand with clear and persuasive illustration. While the university prospectus does not say that this course would be given "by dictation," that phrase is used for several other courses Hegel was offering at the time. And we can imagine that the new professor, uncertain with this first exposure to the university scene after close to ten years in the newspaper business and teaching secondary school, was moving cautiously.[4]

Karl Hegel's notes are quite different. Rather than being written while the lecture was going on, Karl followed the practice, adopted by the more serious students, of taking notes at the time and then reworking these into a flowing prose text in his study afterwards. As well, Hegel had abandoned the method of dictation for a freer lecture style, offering illustrations, turning aside for footnotes and observations, anticipating themes to be developed later. Here we have a sense of that comprehensive vivacity which made Hegel such an entrancing lecturer for his students. And the textbook used was the full, expanded version of 1830.

---

3. From Rameil's Introduction to the Lectures of 1831, *V* 10: XLII, fn 35.
4. Hegel's candidacy for the chair at Berlin had been set aside in 1816 because the Prussian authorities were uncertain about his experience in giving full scale university lectures.

It would take us too far afield to follow through the development of the lectures in detail. We can, however, consider one important feature of these notes which we do not find in the more academic *Science of Logic*. As mentioned earlier, the lectures were announced as encompassing both logic and metaphysics. To be sure, Hegel has said that the *Science of Logic* "takes the place of what previously was called metaphysics,"[5] but when we examine the detailed analysis of the various concepts, we seldom move beyond the specific meaning of the terms being discussed. In the lectures, however, Hegel continually talks about how the various concepts, and in particular those which either begin or complete a cycle, can be understood as predicates, describing God—or, if he is talking to students imbued with more abstract language, the absolute. So God can be described as Being, Becoming, Infinite, Being on its own account, Essence, Existence, Actuality, the subjectivity of Conceiving, Life and the absolute Idea. The intermediate terms, which introduce distinctions and then develop into a pattern of mutual interaction, are more partial and restricted, even though they contribute to the more comprehensive predicates.

The language of "the absolute" Hegel has taken over from his colleague from Tübingen and Jena, Schelling, to describe the totality of all that is. By placing his logical discussion of this concept in the Doctrine of Essence, however, he has suggested that it is in some sense limited since it does not incorporate the dynamic subjectivity of conceptual thinking. So he is happier with the term "God." Indeed he claims, in the preface to the *Science of Logic*, that the logic presents us with God as he was before the creation of the world.[6]

Hegel's use of this language in his lectures might simply provide evidence of his concern to avoid the charge of atheism that had ruined, for a time, the career of his predecessor, Fichte.[7] In the early nineteenth century, it was politic to show how philosophy fitted, and did justice to, the conventions of received religion. But more may also be involved. For Hegel wants to say that the concepts explored by the logic capture the essential structure of the universe. This is the way things really are. For all that we are surrounded by the material world of space and time, of individuals and societies, the ultimate core of reality is a structure of meaning which can be investigated and fully understood. Plato had called this significant explanation of all that is the Idea of the Good; and early Christian theologians had suggested that God had created the world out of ideas that he had originally "in his mind." Hegel stands in this tradition.

---

5. *GW* 21: 48; *SL* 63.
6. *GW* 21: 34; *SL* 50.
7. Fichte had claimed that God was nothing but the moral order of the universe. The father of one of his students laid a charge of atheism, and in the resulting furor Fichte was relieved of his post at the University of Jena, though he continued to receive a pension from the state.

As we explore the concepts of pure thought, from the most basic and indeterminate ("being") through the patterns of mutual interaction ("essence") to those of subjectivity ("conceiving") we are rethinking the "thoughts of God." We are articulating those patterns of meaning and significance that underlie the cosmos, and which become explicit in the world of nature, finite spirits and society. These are universal, applying not only to the material and social world, but also to the products of pure thinking itself: concepts, judgements, inferences; images, products of our imagination, and represented conceptualizations.

Traditional metaphysics had attempted to achieve the same results. But it tied up pure thoughts with more determinate content: souls were not simply substances or essences, but tied to concrete human bodies; the cosmos was not simply an intricate structure of meaning, but a realm of space and time, of actual parts and wholes, causes and effects, of appearances and underlying reality; god was a determinate being distinct from the created world, yet ensuring that it fitted into his limiting purposes.

Embedded in all of this traditional discussion lies the reasoning that leads from thought to thought. Conclusions are reached on the basis of thinking alone: whenever contradictions emerge, we must adopt the contrary of their presuppositions; determinate meanings lead us to one set of implications rather than another. But the confusion of these thoughts with more determinate content means that the internal dynamic of pure thought which underlies all such reality was not considered on its own, and led metaphysicians to predict what the actual world was like, rather than exploring its nature using careful observation and scientific tools.

In his lectures, then, Hegel is not simply reworking the material of the traditional metaphysics. Rather than starting from God, the cosmos and the soul, he starts from the realm of pure thoughts. And as he follows its logic from concept to concept, he knows that he is uncovering the inherent structure of all that is—of what makes us humans what we are, of what makes the cosmos function the way it does, and why the totality of all that is can be understood as the meaningful product of a comprehensive subjectivity.

PART VI

Logic and the System

Chapter 19

The Philosophy of Nature

In Hegel's original plan, his system was to include, not only the introductory *Phenomenology of Spirit*, and the three-volume *Science of Logic*, but also a full-fledged *Philosophy of Nature* and a *Philosophy of Spirit*. Once he returned to the university and became enmeshed in the routine of preparing regular lectures on a wide-ranging series of topics—natural science and psychology, politics and economics, history, religion, and art—that grand scheme was abandoned. He did, however, sketch out what would be involved in the full system in the *Encyclopaedia of the Philosophical Sciences in Outline*, a text he revised twice during his Berlin years. So we do have an indication of what he intended to do when he began publishing his "System of the Sciences"[1] in 1807.

There is, however, a major problem in devising a system that includes not only the structures of pure thought, but also the principles of nature and human society. What happens when one moves from concepts such as "being," "actuality," or "syllogism" to a discussion of space and time, matter and movement, electricity and plants? Or indeed of desire and perception, imagination and willed determination, contracts, family life, economics and politics? In these latter disciplines we are talking about what is happening around us—things and events that we cannot anticipate in advance, but only come to know through careful observation and discovery. But talk of a system suggests that one can move from stage to stage using nothing but the resources of disciplined thought. Hegel would seem to be claiming that we can articulate the structure of the whole universe simply by relying on our own reasoning.

Some indeed claim that this is what Hegel has in mind. All he does is introduce into the set of concepts already articulated in the *Logic* a new wrinkle: "otherness," for example, or better "the total realm

---

1. On its original title page, the *Phenomenology of Spirit* is described as only the first part of the full system.

of otherness."[2] Others, however, argue that this move is the fatal flaw in Hegel's philosophy. Hegel's early colleague, Schelling, attacked him for illegitimately jumping across the nasty, broad ditch[3] from pure thought to existence. And the twentieth century philosopher of science, Karl Popper, simply dismissed Hegel as unworthy of respect because he had "deduced" the actual position of the planets while ignoring the recent discovery of a small one (Ceres) between Mars and Jupiter.[4]

There is, however, a way of reading Hegel's transition from the logic to the philosophy of nature that would save him from the charge of presumptuous rationalism. It starts by looking closely at the two texts where he introduces that move.

In the last paragraph of the *Science of Logic* Hegel says that, once we reach the end of the logic with its discussion of method, pure thought has become completely transparent. So there can be no further intellectual transition to another concept in the manner followed by the logic's internal development. Nothing implicit remains to be explicated. At this point the idea (or pure thought) is absolutely sure of, and at peace with, itself; so the only transition possible is, in absolute freedom, to make itself redundant.[5] This involves being open to what comes from outside, rather than seeking to determine it oneself.

In the *Encyclopaedia Logic*, the description becomes more complicated. Since the idea, or fully transparent thought, is absolutely free, it does not simply move on to life, nor allows life to surface in finite cognition. Rather, being absolutely assured of its own nature and status, the idea freely decides to release from itself the moment of its particularity—all the ways thought introduces determination into its starting point—as nature.[6]

We have here two critical phrases: thought "freely makes itself redundant," and thought "decides, with respect to itself, freely to release the immediate idea as its mirror image from itself as nature." This means that there is nothing constraining thought, either from outside, or from its own unnoticed implicit nature. Thought is now not focussing on how the various

---

2. Such a position can be found in some of the contributions to the issue of *The Owl of Minerva* devoted to "Logic, Nature, and Empirical Science," Volume 34, No. 1 (Fall/Winter 2002–03). See in particular those of Edward Harper and Stephen Houlgate.

3. The phrase comes from G. Lessing's pamphlet: "On the Fruit of the Spirit and of Power."

4. See F.W.J. Schelling, *On the History of Modern Philosophy*, translated by Andrew Bowie, (Cambridge: Cambridge University Press, 1994) 155 and K. Popper, *The Open Society and its Enemies* (Princeton: Princeton University Press, 1966) II, 27.

5. *GW* 12: 253; *SL* 843. Hegel's word is *entlassen*, which means "to dismiss," "to make redundant," "to discharge," "to pension off." His innovation is to make this verb reflexive: "to make itself redundant," "to pension itself off."

6. *EL* §244. Although the same German infinitive *sich entlassen* is used in both texts, in the larger *Logic* the reflexive pronoun is in the accusative, so that the idea "releases, discharges or frees" itself. In the *Encyclopaedia*, however, the object of the verb is "the immediate idea as its mirror image," so the reflexive pronoun is in the dative: "*with respect to itself* it freely releases the immediate idea as its mirror image from itself as nature."

moments it has identified in its logical pilgrimage are implicitly related to each other, but allowing each of them to stand on its own, unrelated to the others. In other words, thought is altering the way it approaches its subject matter. By acknowledging how natural determinations will be external and unrelated, philosophy recognizes that it cannot force them to satisfy its own conceptual expectations, but must observe, carefully, just how they emerge. It no longer thinks, but intuits. And what it intuits is not itself thought, but nature.

Unregulated intuition, however, can make little sense of the booming, buzzing confusion that is around us. So thought is not completely passive. It directs its attention by defining what kind of otherness is to be considered at any particular point. It identifies which determination it is, for the moment, interested in. And it notices the particular forms this "kind of otherness" takes—forms that are not themselves anticipated by thought. Once it has observed these contingencies, thought can then consider their influence on the way nature's externality is to be conceived. This involves setting up another "kind of otherness"—a new concept that incorporates the recently discovered novelties—that can serve as a platform for further observation.

In other words, when Hegel comes to his philosophy of nature, he relies on pure thought to focus its attention; and he uses thought's speculative powers to integrate what it discovers with concepts already developed. But he cannot predict in advance, by any form of pure thought, just what disciplined intuition will encounter once it looks for a particular isolated determination.

The *Philosophy of Nature* starts when thought is open to a nature that is a complete realm of external relations; things are not connected by any meaning or implication, but simply stand outside each other. Observation discovers that this "abstract universality of externality" is space, which turns out to allow our thought to discriminate within it three dimensions, and to differentiate point from line, from plane, and from solid.

Thought now returns. These different moments are the negation of each other, and one wonders what it would be like to have an externality that on its own explicitly incorporates such negation. Observation discovers that time satisfied this requirement. Indeed in its movement from the existing present to the non-existing past, and from the non-existing future to the existing present, time captures the same structure that the logic identified in its concept "becoming."

Unlike the shifts from "being" to "nothing" and back again, the "presents" of time simply disappear into an indifferent past. Each one simply leaves its trace as an independent moment externally related to others in space. So just as reflection on space led us to time, reflection on time leads us back to space. We have one of those circles which speculative thought loves to exploit. So thought now learns that a space which has its own past is a place; and the temporal shift from a past place to a present one involves movement. The integration of place and motion emerges in nature as matter.

By reading Hegel's *Philosophy of Nature* as a dialogue of this sort between the expectations and speculations of thought and the givens of radical observation, we can see how Hegel could distinguish between the concepts of mechanism, chemism and life that he places in the *Logic* and his discussions of mechanics, chemistry and organics in the philosophy of nature. "Mechanism," "chemism," and "life" are ways thought organizes its thinking about any objects whatever, whether those objects be things in the world or pure concepts. As such, each one has its own internal logic: mechanism developing the tension between stronger and weaker forces; chemism requiring a mediating catalyst; life requiring a process of adaptation to the environment. These results follow logically from the internal requirements of the initial concept.

But when we come to the philosophy of nature these particular determinations have a life of their own. At the point where we look for mechanical systems, we find things like inertia, weight, gravity, and the free movement of the planets around their centre. Chemical processes convert metals into oxides, acids and alkalis, and these in turn produce neutral salts, while each combination has as its counterpart the separation of components that had previously been closely associated. The earth represents a non-living organism, and plants and animals articulate the dynamic of life in diverse ways.

So the movement through the philosophy of nature follows a quite different path from that spelled out in the domaine of pure thought. From mechanics one moves into the physics of light, earth, air, fire and water; specific weight, cohesion, sound and warmth; magnetism and electricity. Only then do we arrive at chemistry. And instead of going via teleology to the concept of life, the philosophy of nature shifts to non-living organisms before beginning to introduce elements that embody the nature of life.

Nonetheless logical thinking has an important role to play. Otherwise it would not be a *philosophy* of nature. Thought identifies just what is legitimately to be looked for at any particular stage of the investigation. And it does this by integrating what it has discovered from nature in the previous stage with its own conceptual arsenal—not only the concepts previously explored in the *Logic* but also any earlier construction developed in the course of the *Philosophy of Nature* itself. This requires careful discrimination to ensure that no illegitimate sense is being introduced, and that one's observations are appropriate to the concepts being "applied." But thought on its own does not anticipate or predict the form those observations will take, and what in fact will emerge in nature.

This rigorous separation between thought and nature has another implication. Thought, as we have seen, has its own internal dynamic of development. One concept leads over to another and vice versa; reflection can look back over the whole process and consider it in its totality; understanding can articulate how the various moments are interrelated and integrated into a single new concept. But nature is the realm of external relations. If things do interact among themselves this will have to be discovered. Even when we do find interaction, the externality and impotence of nature makes it incapable of integrating this complex dynamic into a new form of existence. Any integrating move is done by philosophical thinking, as it takes the results of observation and brings them together with its own treasury of concepts. This means that, for Hegel, there is no evolution in nature—no process where natural forms metamorphose on their own into other forms. At one level he takes this position simply because science had not yet shown the viability of evolution; he was not prepared to tell nature what it should be like. At another level, however, it follows from his conception of nature as completely other than thought: externality rather than internal relations; powerless rather than fully self-determining. Thought alone has the power of integration. Even when we find living organisms in nature that are able to assimilate their environment into living individuality, they do not have the ability to learn from their failures and adapt to new situations. Something further would be required to explain how one efficient type of organism could be transformed into one of a completely different sort. That, says Hegel, is found when we move from the externality of nature to a form of life that is centred and adaptive—what he calls spirit.

Hegel's philosophy of nature has not received much attention from subsequent thinkers. Unlike the *Phenomenology* or his political philosophy it does not provide a rich lode of insights that can be mined for understanding human affairs. It is, after all, limited by the fact that he knows only the science of his own time. And his philosophical preconceptions, moulded by the German scientific community, had an influence on how he interpreted the experimental data. His analysis, however, does reveal the way thought interacts with observation in our understanding of nature. It is the preconceptions of thought which determine where we look and what we are looking for. And any explanation that seeks to integrate those observations with our general understanding of the world requires the use of a conceptual arsenal, which can be adopted either unthinkingly or with careful reflection. Little attention has been paid to the role thought plays in the scientific enterprise. By making his discussion of nature a sequel to his *Logic* Hegel has gone some way to correcting that imbalance.

Chapter 20

The Philosophy of Spirit and Philosophy of Right

Hegel calls the third part of his system the "Philosophy of Spirit." He prefers the term "spirit" to either the traditional "soul" or the earlier English translation "mind" because the spirit not only thinks but also wills and acts. In addition, it presupposes nature and incorporates it into its life: both as the body which gives it birth and the environment within which it functions.

Within the *Encyclopaedia* system, spirit emerges as a new stage once thought reflects on the nature of animal life. An animal is an organism that can reproduce itself, yet is susceptible to illness and ultimately death. Speculative thought combines this sense of a living self-reproducing organism together with the process of dying, and it comes up with the thought of a being that is able to learn from death, and so go beyond it. Such a being would not then be restricted to the particular form it happens to have, but can face up to its limitations and transcend them. Unlike nature in Hegel's view, spirit is amenable to metamorphosis.

It is not just individual humans who embody the structure of spirit. For people interact to create communities which rise above the particular existence of their members and have an ongoing life of their own. "Spirit" captures this sphere of human interaction as a whole in a way that "soul" and "mind" could never do. Indeed, once we take account of the full range of human life, we notice how it continually incorporates into its purview reality as a whole. So Hegel includes within his discussion of spirit those spheres of human life that explore how it fits into the ultimate nature of things: world history, art, religion, and philosophy.

On turning from nature to spirit the role of logical thought changes. Nature, for Hegel, is the realm of externality. For scientific purposes, each determinate feature can be isolated on its own without affecting the others. So thought concentrates on a particular feature and observes the way it exists in the external world; any further integration into more complex structures is its own work, setting the stage for new investigations to see if they also can be found in nature. Even animal life, with its ability to reproduce itself as a centred organism, can never go beyond its specific limitations. Each species (in Hegel's pre-evolutionary view) is a self-contained cycle of recurrent individuals which thrive and then pass away. The process of integrating specific details into more comprehensive thoughts happens only within the philosophical system.

Spirit, however, can overreach its own limitations, and thereby transform itself; simpler stages are incorporated into larger, more complex ones. When we look for the forms spirit takes in the world around us, then, we always find them embedded in rich complexity: intelligent, focused individuals who work together to create families and market economies and nation states. The most elementary expressions of spirit in particular are never found in isolation.

So whenever thought wants to observe the way spirit functions, it already has an integrated individual within an integrated community. Its task is not to formulate, speculatively, a complex concept. Rather it needs to analyze carefully: to identify in thought the most basic forms of spiritual existence and consider how they function and interact to produce more developed levels of self-conscious life. Philosophy needs to ensure that more advanced, and more complicated, phenomena are not introduced into the analysis before they are required by the demands of careful thought. In other words, the critical task is that of understanding—of individuating the various components of spiritual life and placing them in their proper position and order. To do that well, however, we must also establish how the inevitable dialectic leads to those more integrated structures with which we are familiar.

The logic provides some basic perspectives that govern our investigation. Under the concept of "cognition"[1] it has shown how life requires that subjectivity and objectivity come to correspond with each other. This follows two patterns: the subject seeks to model the object ("the idea of the true"); and it seeks to remould the object to its purposes ("the idea of the good"). Only when the two opposite processes are integrated into a single, more complex, dynamic is satisfaction reached. We shall find that this general structure governs Hegel's whole analysis of subjective spirit.

---

1. See Chapter 15. Hegel himself draws the connection between "cognition" and the three disciplines of anthropology, phenomenology and psychology. See *SL* 78off; *GW* 12: 197ff: "Now [in contrast to life] this Idea is spirit. In this context we may once more remark that spirit is here [in the section on cognition] considered in the form that belongs to this Idea as logical. For it has other shapes as well that may be mentioned in passing; in these it falls to be considered in the concrete sciences of spirit, namely as *soul, consciousness and spirit as such.*"

Anthropology

Hegel starts with individual "finite spirits" (as he calls us) and isolates the most primitive modes by which we rise above the limitations of animal existence. Anthropology identifies the way fledgling spirit (or "soul" as Hegel calls it at this stage) becomes sensitive to its immediate natural setting: its environmental and genetic situation, as well as the natural alterations of aging, sexual maturity, sleeping and waking. Yet the soul is not simply passive. It has its own "genius" and develops an incipient sense of itself; in course of time it develops habits by which it moulds the natural givens of the body and its setting so that they are incorporated into its own life. By combining sensitivity and habitual routine it realizes its potential, and becomes actual.

In normal life we do not find the anthropological levels that Hegel has analyzed in any pure form. They have been absorbed into the richer life of consciousness and spirit. Yet they do surface from time to time, usually as forms of mental illness or deprivation, when individuals regress to more primitive forms of what Hegel calls self-feeling, or sense of self.[2] While forms of mental illness do provide clues to these elementary levels, however, they do not always present them in an unambiguous way, since they frequently retain traces of the more developed life from which they have regressed. As a result, to identify these most primitive forms of spiritual life, the philosophy of spirit must isolate in thought the most basic ways we respond to our world, and show how some are more complex forms of others; how sensitivity is balanced by the habits through which we fit the world to our sense of self; and how, together, the two processes interact to provide the foundation for consciousness.

Phenomenology

The stable "soul" that is the product of habitual behaviour is now able to differentiate itself from its surrounding world, which thus becomes an object of consciousness. So anthropology is succeeded by phenomenology, the discipline that explores how, first, consciousness adapts to the world of objects and, then, how self-consciousness incorporates that world into its self-certainty. At this point Hegel introduces themes that he has already discussed in the *Phenomenology of Spirit*. In the earlier work, he was primarily concerned with our quest for knowledge; this pushed him beyond the spheres of consciousness and self-consciousness to explore some of the basic categories of reason, and the knowledge claims of self-confident

---

2. Hegel's biographers point out that his life was not untouched by mental illness. Both his sister, and his friend, the poet Hölderlin, ended their lives requiring institutional care. And in a letter written in 1810 Hegel admitted that he had suffered from "hypochondria to the point of exhaustion." *Hegel: The Letters*, tr. C. Butler & C. Seiler (Bloomington: Indiana University Press, 1984) 561.

societies. Now, within the *Encyclopaedia Philosophy of Spirit*, he simply wants to identify the ways by which consciousness tries to conform its conceptions to reflect its environment, and then how self-consciousness seeks to come to terms with itself by overreaching the world around it.

In both works, he moves through immediate sensation, perception and then understanding to the point where we learn that we are as much involved in forming our apprehension of the world as are the givens we confront. Similarly the self becomes conscious of itself through desire, recognition, death, the work of a frightened slave and the enjoyment of a dominating master, only to learn that it knows itself most adequately when in resignation it accepts the way the world restricts and limits its freedom.[3] In both works, then, we have a double transition—from object to self, and from self to object—which then becomes integrated into a single perspective wherein thoughts are able to characterize both self and world—the stage Hegel calls reason.

In the 1830 *Philosophy of Spirit*, that achievement simply provides the foundation for the next level of analysis; in the 1807 *Phenomenology* with its interest in secure knowledge, Hegel pushes further. In its quest for certainty, reason applies shared categories, first drawn from the world of objects, then drawn from the world of selves, and finally integrating these two reciprocal processes into the norms that govern how individual selves interact with their world. That this achievement cannot do justice to the quest for truth forces the argument to move further, first to social contexts in which no single principle governs human interaction, but rather tensions between contrary claims articulate the complexities of the social order. Once this exploration of the knowledge claims made by spirit in its communal forms proves to be limited and incomplete, we move on to religion, where humans seek to come to terms with the implicit order of the cosmos. As a final step, absolute knowing, which is, after all, the ultimate quest of the *Phenomenology of Spirit*, integrates the self-knowledge acquired through our social development with the insight we have received from religion concerning the nature of universe.

However, the superstructure of the *Phenomenology of Spirit*, in which the quest for certainty pushes beyond the levels of consciousness and self-consciousness, is not relevant to the task undertaken within the *Encyclopaedia*. In our present context we are not concerned with knowing absolutely, but simply with identifying the various levels of spiritual life that contribute to the normal functioning of human beings.

---

3. The earlier work pushed this analysis of self-consciousness further into the self-knowledge of the Stoics and Skeptics, and the agony of the unhappy consciousness, which seeks to mortify itself so that it can identify completely with an unchanging other.

Psychology

So we reach the next stage, where we are confident of our essential bond with the environing world. Hegel makes this form of self-conscious existence the proper domain of "spirit," and psychology the appropriate discipline. At this stage, "intellect" governs the quest for the "true," while "will" seeks to realize the "good." In fact, the parallel to the concept of cognition goes further, for intuition introduces analysis, while representation, recollection, imagination and memory adopt various forms of synthesis, and thought endeavours to integrate the two. On the other hand, passion, inclination and thoughtful intentions seek to make the world conform to our will. Once the energy of the will is combined with an intelligent grasp of the world through rational thought, the individual transcends his or her limitations and becomes self-determining, or free.

By this time we can easily identify the stages of analysis Hegel describes: intuition, imagination, memory and inclination. To be sure, when we consider things casually, we often fail to distinguish the recollection of images from the memory of meaningful signs, or the intuition of what is directly in front of us from the representations that collect together repeated impressions from both past and present. But once the distinctions are drawn, we can recognize that the various activities have quite different functions. So it is easier for the discriminations that result from philosophical analysis to find confirmation in our experience than it was in Hegel's anthropology. And we can recognize how the complex beings we turn out to be join together into one all the various levels that thought has put asunder.

The Philosophy of Right

However, as individuals develop freedom and self-determination they have an impact on other individuals, and these impose new, and more intricate restrictions on who we are. No longer can philosophy simply focus on the individual soul, consciousness or intelligent will. It must consider what happens when finite spirits interact, using their ability to both think and implement their intentions. So the philosophy of spirit turns from the subjective realm of what makes us individuals to the objective realm of public affairs.

When Hegel reached Berlin he took the discussion of objective spirit from his *Encyclopaedia* and expanded its original 55 paragraphs into a much more elaborate text, involving 360 paragraphs, in his *Basic Outline for the Philosophy of Right*. Because it explores the fabric of both political and civil society and has given rise to conservative, as well as liberal and socialist ideologies, this work has taken its place beside the earlier *Phenomenology of Spirit* as a primary focus of recent interest in Hegel's thought. Our task here is not to explore its political legacy, but to suggest what role the logic plays in organizing its content.

Hegel isolates our appropriation of objects as the most elementary public action. The initial purpose of property is its free use; but when, over time, we do not use it, we find that our right of possession lapses. Since there is no unlimited right to property we enter into contracts to exchange property we do not need for the property of others. Contracts rely on the trustworthiness of those involved, but people are free to betray trust, resulting in fraud and crime.

This analysis starts from a simple human action that involves both will and intention. It explores what follows from this action, and identifies those results that are not what was intended—the loss of possession through the failure to use. Then thought identifies contracts as a way of resolving this difficulty, only to notice that contracts can fail because of deliberate deception. Hegel is here showing how the sphere of abstract right fits into a pattern that resembles the logical method, and hopes, thereby, to show its rational foundation.

The flaws that deception reveals in contractual law require, then, an analysis of the other side of human behaviour, subjective morality. But here, too, when we isolate what happens in this sphere we discover a dialectic that produces the opposite of what we wanted. For the best and most carefully thought-out actions do not always produce good results; and we frequently end up being responsible for events that were not at all intended.

The next step in Hegel's philosophical analysis is to look at those public spheres where objective agreements and subjective intentions are integrated into an ongoing way of life. Once again he starts with the most basic social setting of the family, based on the subjective bonds of affection and responsibility. And once again the dynamic of social life results in its ultimate demise as children grow up and become independent members of a larger society. The economic independence of civil society, in its turn, requires ever more intricate interconnections through the division of labour, courts to adjudicate disputes, authorities to establish accepted standards of human behaviour, and corporations, both political and commercial, which integrate a number of people into more productive units.

Once again we have a double process, where the family, integrated by mutual affection, breaks apart into independent individuals; and the collective of individuals acting in their own interest develops integrating social structures. The institution that integrates its independent members through a mutual commitment to its defining culture is not civil society, however, but the state. Patriotism introduces subjective bonds like those that hold the family together; the constitution ensures that the interests of the various economic factions are adequately represented in its decisions and laws.

The logical analysis goes further. For states enter into relationships which can involve both the conflict of wars and the satisfaction of mutual interests through treaties. A comprehensive understanding of this dynamic realm of international relations is provided by world history, which thinks back over the way nations have come to be and passed away and can discern in that rhythm a rational pattern.

There is, of course, much more detail to Hegel's analysis than has been provided here. But we can understand why this discussion develops the way it does once we connect it to his *Logic*. Families, economic society, states, international relations and world history are all around us. The role of philosophy is to analyze their makeup to discover the rational structures they embody. And by "rational" Hegel means nothing more than the process where a simple, immediate beginning initiates a process that leads to the opposite of what was initially involved. When we try to rectify this one-sidedness by starting from a contrary beginning, we find that a similar process leads us back to something like the original starting point. So we bring the two together to see what kinds of social phenomena involve the mutual interaction of the two processes.

Ultimately all human activity occurs in political structures that are prey to the currents of history. The task of reflective analysis is to show how simple elements of this totality, once isolated by thought and action, lead over to contrary kinds of results; and how various movements of this sort provide the corrective for each other, and so have come to be combined in new, more complex, social forms. Hegel's social analysis is designed to show that what is rational in fact becomes actual; and the actual itself is, in principle, rational.[4]

But the *Philosophy of Right* is not only a study of the rationality of the world. It is also an exploration of genuine freedom. Freedom means many things: it means coming to terms with, and accepting, one's own limitations ("knowing one's self" as Apollo's oracle said); it means rejecting what is already there and striking out to do something new; it means acting without political and social constraints; it means participating in the governments of one's local community and nation; it means self-determination.

All these many dimensions of freedom are captured within the explanatory pattern of reason. Coming to terms with one's own limitations is the same as understanding the point from which we begin. Rejecting what is already there declares that the status quo is one-sided and needs to be balanced by conflicting claims. Acting without political and social constraints presupposes stable social structures that are limited in their range of application and allow disunion. Participating in government can only occur where political institutions make decisions by incorporating the contributions of individual members, with their particular interests and concerns—

---

4. This, of course, is the famous aphorism found in the Preface to the *Philosophy of Right* (page xix of the original edition).

by integrating particulars and singulars into a comprehensive whole. And we determine ourselves when we not only act and contribute to the social whole, but also accept responsibility for what results and integrate that into our new self-understanding and identity.

Not only are the patterns of freedom and reason the same. They are interrelated. For we are not really free when we do not know what we are doing, or when we do not understand how our action fits into a larger perspective. Nor do we really understand if we have not taken account of what happens when we put thought into practice. To be really free, we need to comprehend the actual world in which we are acting, whether we are rejecting or maintaining it. And we need to take account of all the results, both promising and destructive, of our actions. By bringing together conceptual thought and willed action in this way, we satisfy philosophy's ideal.

Chapter 21

Logic and the Lectures on History, Art, Religion, and Philosophy

Hegel concludes his *Encyclopaedia Philosophy of Spirit* with a discussion of "Absolute Spirit," which covers art, religion and philosophy. These three spheres of human activity, as well as the full range of world history, share a common characteristic: their purpose is to look at human life as a whole. And since logical thought is able to comprehend the dynamic of difference and reconciliation, it was natural for a philosopher to show how these spheres of human life reveal the ultimate nature of things—the way spiritual life is able to transcend all limitations.

Hegel gradually began to develop lecture courses on these four topics. He started lecturing on the history of philosophy while still in Jena, and added a course on aesthetics when in Heidelberg; then in the early 1820s he introduced lectures on the philosophy of religion and the philosophy of world history for his Berlin students. In every case he was breaking new ground. To cover the whole range of philosophy from the pre-Socratics to his immediate predecessors in one course demanded a comprehensive organising perspective. The same applied to his discussions of all the art forms and their history; the whole panorama of religion from the animism of Africa and the north, through the traditional religions of Asia, the Near East, and the Mediterranean to the Protestantism of northern Europe; and the range of human history, reaching back to the earliest known records of political and social activity. All these spheres of human life are grist for the mill of philosophy. For Hegel claims that any human activity whatever is rational, and thus provides evidence for the ultimate rationality of the universe.

In other words, Hegel was not simply pre-empting topics that were the proper concern of historians, whether of political, artistic or religious practices. He was claiming that one could study these spheres "scientifically." Philosophy could show the rational principles that governed both their history and their structure.

Our concern here is not to talk about the content of these lectures. That content Hegel shared with his sources—other academics, travellers to the remote ends of the earth and current journals. Rather we shall focus on what he meant in saying that this material could be organized according to the structures of reason.

We should note, first, that Hegel was not committed to a single logical pattern. He revised the organization of both his aesthetics lectures and those on the philosophy of religion—sometimes quite significantly.[1] While he was convinced that a rational pattern could be found; he was not committed to any particular formulation; he was ready to change his mind.

History and philosophy are not so amenable to structural revision. One cannot change the course of events, already past, nor can one reorder the sequence of philosophical systems as they emerge over time. But it is precisely here, in the ongoing flow of history, that Hegel finds the rationality of the life that spirit leads. For spirit, as we have seen, is what does not disappear when death arrives, but re-emerges in a transformed state. So a particular culture pushes itself to the limit, only to decline and falter, leaving its failure as a lesson for future generations.

Any culture reacts to its predecessor, vibrant and vital in its discovery of a new principle of life. While the contingencies of geography, of climate and of historical circumstance influence and determine its development, these very contingencies become incorporated into its self-understanding. A sense of destiny, implicit in its religion, gradually becomes more articulate and consciously defined, finding expression in social custom and political institutions. The culture thus acquires a complete integration of its inherent genius. At this point philosophers come on the scene, showing how everything fits together. But by making the genius of the culture fully explicit, philosophy initiates the decline. For reflective thought shows not only what are its strengths but also its limitations. Self-conscious life senses that more is involved than what has already been accomplished. And so spirit reacts instinctively and passionately, introducing dispersion and conflict and leading to dissolution and decay. In this way dominant societies emerge and decline, to be followed by others, in other regions, who take their place on the world stage.

For Hegel, reason, with its pattern of determinate understanding, dialectical difference and speculative integration provides an appropriate means for comprehending the truth inherent in history. After all, the *Phenomenology* has shown that reason is but the distilled essence of self-conscious life— its abstracted principle. Philosophical thought can trace how chance

---

1. One can see this particularly in the three volume edition of the *Lectures on the Philosophy of Religion*, edited by Walter Jaeschke and translated into English by Peter C. Hodgson and his colleagues (Berkeley and Los Angeles: University of California Press, 1984–87).

circumstances are incorporated and resisted, why cultures rise and fall. It can recognize in the total pattern of world history a development, as national life progresses from less articulate to more comprehensive forms, not only in each society, but throughout world history generally; how the full development of any position leads inevitably to its contrary; how the next generation can learn from previous failures.

By coming to terms with the restrictions and limitations that frustrate life, spirit incorporates them into its own dynamic. They are no longer submitted to as the inevitable givens of fate, but resources that can be exploited to accomplish new purposes. So the philosopher can also view human history as a process of developing freedom. As each new culture encounters new limitations, while overreaching and overcoming those that condemned its predecessor, the human spirit becomes more effective in determining itself, less prey to alien, determining influences. Humans expand the range of their freedom.

With this in mind, Hegel schematically differentiates the historical epochs by saying that, in the ancient East, one was free; in the classical world of Greece and Rome, some are free; but in the modern "Germanic" world of northern Europe and its colonial extensions, all are free.

This "rational" pattern that governs the way human history moves through time is equally effective in specific areas of human culture: art, religion and philosophy. Philosophy in particular can be seen as a developmental pattern, exploring particular themes, only to come to the limits of their possibilities and shifting to other, complementary ones. Greek and Roman philosophy investigated the way conceptual thinking comprehends reality. In the Presocratics this focused on the underlying principles of the objective world; with the Sophists and Socrates it turned to subjective themes: morality, knowledge and political order. Plato and Aristotle brought these two contrary approaches together, but without a systematic integrating principle. When the Stoics and Epicureans each sought to find such a principle, they were confronted by the Skeptics, who denied that one was possible. It was the Neo-Platonists, and in particular Proclus, who brought these latter two strategies together by recognising that unity, limitation and the unlimited each have distinctive functions, yet are integrated into an all-encompassing totality.

The intellectual achievement of Neo-Platonism remained an abstraction of thought. Christianity, while also stressing the complexity of an integrated trinity, added the conviction that the ultimate ground of rationality had become actual and would continue to do so, through the exercise of freedom. Modern philosophy took off from this insight when Bacon, on one side, appealed to the givens of experience and Jakob Boehme advanced an integrating speculative insight. Spinoza and Descartes stressed the importance of the universality of thought; Hobbes, Locke, Leibniz and Hume stressed, in contrast, the importance of the particular. It was Kant and his successors, Fichte and Schelling, who brought these two strands together into a single perspective.

So philosophy's history also shows the same pattern of abstract emphasis, dialectical division and integrating speculation that we found embedded in the history of cultures and nations.

With art and religion it is not so easy to adopt a simple historical approach. For the great works of art from the past still generate a powerful aesthetic response; and religious traditions that flourished long ago still exercise their influence and fascination in the contemporary world. So the historical story has to be balanced with other, systematic, considerations.

In his *Lectures on Aesthetics* Hegel identifies three great periods of human artistic achievement. In the symbolic period, the ideal struggled to find material embodiment. Architecture in particular was used to evoke the sublime beyond. In classical Greece and Rome beauty found its most complete expression. Sculpture captured in stone the ideal unity of spirit, whereas epic, lyric and drama transformed static beauty into something dynamic, incorporating subjectivity. A full exploration of subjectivity, however, disrupts the union of physical and spiritual found in classical art. The modern, romantic, period uses art to give expression to the ultimates of spiritual life in a way that is not restricted to its material form. Painting with its use of perspective, music and poetry all suggest what is not immediately present.

But it is not enough simply to paint this history. For each particular art form has is own inherent pattern and possibility. Initially Hegel included his discussion of the three historical "stages" or "forms" of art under the theme of *universality*, after he had explored the concept of beauty. Then he talked about architecture and sculpture, painting, music, and poetry as the *particular* ways in which this universal pattern found expression. Implicit was the suggestion that the individual moment would include *singular* works of art. In his final series of lectures, however, Hegel changed the organization (and his editor, Heinrich Hotho, adopted it when preparing the second edition of the *Lectures* even though he incorporated material from the earlier lectures). Now the *universal* moment simply focused on the idea of beauty as the ideal; symbolic, classical and romantic became the *particular* forms that this ideal took; and the various arts, from architecture to the novel, assumed the role of the individual or *singular*.

In pointing beyond the materiality of the art work to its ultimate significance, art itself suggests that only religion can do justice to the ultimate ideality of spiritual life. So Hegel situates art as a first, intuitive approach to the ultimate that is to be developed through the more representational forms of religious thought and practice, and to reach its completion in the conceptual universality of philosophical thought.

As in the *Aesthetics*, there remains in his *Lectures on the Philosophy of Religion* a certain historical (and geographical) framework. In discussing the particular traditions, Hegel starts from tribal religions of Africa and the far north, then moves to China, India, Persia, Egypt, Palestine, Greece, Rome, and finally to northern Europe. But a more ideological program determines his organization. As elsewhere, he starts with the concept of religion—its *universal*, theoretical structure. The various religions of Africa, Asia and the Mediterranean are then considered as *particular* forms of this concept, each one focused on a particular aspect: the union of humans with the surrounding cosmos is emphasized in tribal, Chinese and Indian religion; the contrast between what is contingently present and the essential beyond emerges in the religions of the Mediterranean: suggested in Persia and Egypt, diversity reigning in Greece in contrast with the sublime unity of God in Judaism (and Islam), and all assembled together by Rome under the mantle of expediency, but so superficially that it immediately disintegrates into triviality and brutality.

One can see from the various sets of lectures that Hegel continued to experiment with the conceptual organization of this range of traditions. Judaism in particular shifted from being the complement of Greek religion to accompanying the Parsee religion as a stage introductory to Egypt, well before the discussion of Greece and Rome. At different times he would correlate the various kinds of arguments for the existence of God with different traditions.

In every lecture series, however, the integration of all the diversity came in the final section, called "The Consummate Religion," which discusses (primarily Protestant) Christianity. For Hegel, Christianity is the *individual* religion which incorporates and makes explicit all the diverse features that make up the concept of religion. The lecture series culminates here, so that even though Hinduism, Buddhism, Islam and Judaism (along with others) continue to be alive and dynamic in the world, they all serve primarily as precursors to the religion of northern Europe. But Christianity does not fit the sense of "singular" as an immediate object of reference. Rather, Hegel can introduce it as the logical completion of the triad, universal/particular/singular, only by adopting a second reading of "singular" introduced in the 1830 *Encyclopaedia Logic*.[2] There the singular is a totality which incorporates into a unity all of the universal determinations. "The consummate religion" (as Hegel calls it) completes the picture only because it incorporates *all* the critical themes present in the other religions.

We do not find, then, a uniform pattern in the various lecture series that would define what makes them "scientific" in contrast with the more unstructured approaches of the conventional historian, whether of politics, art, religion or philosophy. All of them, certainly, betray to some extent the

---

2. See Chapter 17.

dynamic pattern over time of starting with an implicit principle, working it out in the concrete life of a people to the point where it is fully articulate, having this flourishing trigger its own decline, and being replaced with a new principle. All history betrays this implicit logic of spiritual life.

But Hegel wants an additional systematic structure. Superimposed on art history's sequence, he introduces the pattern of the *general* concept of beauty, the *particular* forms it takes, and the *individual* arts. With respect to the history of religion, he moves from the *general* concept of religion to the *particular* religions in a sequence from natural religion through the religions of beauty and sublimity, and concludes with the discussion of Christianity as the *consummation* of the whole development.[3] Both discussions adopt the tripartite division of universal (the concept), particular, and singular. But "singular" appears to have several meanings. In his *Aesthetics*, the "singular" is either the individual works of art, dispersed here and there, or the various modes of artistic expression; in his *Philosophy of Religion*, the "singular" is one particular tradition which integrates all the various elements and themes of the previous discussion into a single, comprehensive totality.

The *Logic*, then, plays a role in determining the framework for his lectures. It is what leads him into introducing world history, aesthetics, religion and even the history of philosophy into the philosophical curriculum. But it does not appear to have been a straightjacket into which the phenomena of human life was forced. It takes different forms, depending on the subject matter; and it was revisable. Each time he offered a particular course, he rethought its organization. Logical categories provide some kind of organizing principle, but they are amenable to further reflection, that takes account of the material being discussed, or of differing insights into what was critical to the topic in question. Hegel's lectures, given orally over time, were themselves subject to the historical dialectic that he describes. Only when they were collected into a single story by his editors and published as the words of "the immortalized" did they come to be ossified into a definitive structure.

---

3. Hegel does not do the same in his discussion of the history of philosophy. For the systematic development of philosophical principles is to be found in his *Logic*. This is why one can find parallels between the concepts discussed in the *Logic* and the positions of particular philosophers throughout history.

Chapter 22

Absolute Spirit

In looking at the lectures on world history, aesthetics, religion and the history of philosophy, we have covered what Hegel said about those spheres of human existence where we seek a comprehensive understanding. But we have not shown how these fit into his system. That question he takes up in the final section of his *Encyclopaedia of the Philosophical Sciences*, entitled "Absolute Spirit." Through the whole development from anthropology and psychology to right, morality, family, society and the state, spirit has become more conscious of its own nature as active. When, in the *Philosophy of Right*, one surveys the panorama of world history one begins to grasp the realm of spirit as a whole. But even then it is spread out over vast dimensions of time. Just as conceptual thinking can take a synthesis of dynamic processes and integrate them into a single thought, however, spirit can integrate its understanding of this whole into a single relationship.

Religion has been that sphere of human life in which we relate to the ultimate ground or explanation of the cosmos. That relationship has adopted at least three different forms. In the first place, we create an object which embodies our intuitive insights into the nature of reality. Art, and in particular the art of classical Greece, integrates spirit and the natural elements of the world in this way. In the second place, we set out our thoughts about the ultimate in discourse, thoughts which distill our response to those ways that the transcendent has become manifest in human life. Such representations have as their counterpart willed action, so that religious traditions have developed not only doctrine but religious practice. In the third place, we think in order to understand the way things are—not only distinguishing the various components but articulating how they are related to each other within a comprehensive perspective. This is the accomplishment of philosophy. Absolute spirit, then, finds its human expression in art, religion and philosophy.

This division betrays its own rational structure. The intuitions that motivate the artist and inspire the aesthetic audience are immediate and direct—a simple, yet all-encompassing insight. Religion breaks up such insights into elements of doctrine and diverse practices, each of which describes some part of the truth, but leaves the total picture only as an implicit, felt faith. Philosophy brings together the diversity present in religion with the unity of art to articulate an intricate and complex totality. The simple unity of the universal, the diversity of particulars, and the integrated totality of the singular structures our relationships with ultimate reality[1]

But Hegel introduces further logical considerations into what he says, schematically, about both religion and philosophy.

In the *Encyclopaedia* he is not interested in exploring the whole historical panorama of art, religion, or philosophy. As noted above, he focuses his discussion of art on Greece, where beauty—in both sculpture and drama—was the ultimate expression of our human relationship to the beyond. The earlier symbolic stage pointed to a sublimity yearned for but never reached; while the later romantic stage used the objective forms of art to suggest a realm of spirit that always transcended any particular manifestation; neither use art to provide direct access to the essence of all things. In the same way, religion in the *Encyclopaedia* refers to revealed religion—Christianity, not the various particular religions that populate the world. And philosophy, it would appear, is the philosophy articulated by Hegel himself.

As well, the discussion of revealed religion is organized according to the language of concept, judgement and syllogism. God in himself is the universal concept, internally articulated into a trinity but ultimately a spiritual unity, the power able to create both the heavens and the earth. When he does create he introduces particular differences—not only between created and creator, but also in the diversity that lacks the internal unity of the divine. This is an act of judgement; and the differences are radicalized when the created others develop independent centres of thought and action that resist and reject the divine order.

The plurality and division of the created order is overcome through three syllogisms of reconciliation. In the first, the particularity of division and death mediates between an individual who integrates the divine and the human and his universal presence as spirit. Like the Barbara syllogism, particularity is a middle term between singular and universal. In the second syllogism, what is thus reported about the singular individual mediates between the diverse particulars of dispersed humanity and their incorporation into the universal spirit that is God. Like induction where singular mediates between particularity and universality, the unique story

---

1. I have been avoiding the term "God," since that is primarily a religious word, whereas art might talk about "the Spiritual" and philosophy about "Truth," or "the Absolute."

of a God-man who dies and thus becomes universal spirit takes the resistant independence of differentiated humans, and incorporates it into the universal life of the Holy Spirit. Finally, it is this universal spirit of God that brings together the individual who overcame the finitude of life through the crucifixion and the many particular people who have been incorporated into the life of the church. Like the disjunctive syllogism the universal mediates between singular and particular.

These three syllogisms, Hegel says, make up a single complex syllogism where the life of spirit mediates itself. And it is in grasping the integrated quality of this totality that the way is opened to a fully philosophic comprehension.

The pattern of three syllogisms reappears in Hegel's final section on philosophy—or at least it did in two of the three editions of the *Encyclopaedia*. In the first edition of 1817, this triad marked the culmination of the argument, as if to summarize everything that has gone before in the Logic, the Philosophy of Nature and the Philosophy of Spirit. In the second edition of 1827 they were omitted, even though the *Encyclopaedia* as a whole had been expanded by a hundred additional paragraphs. Three years later, in 1830, they reappeared, although with a new introductory sentence which says that the appearance of philosophy establishes further developments—as if the system is not completely closed.

The first of these syllogisms has the logical as its starting point and nature as its middle. The result is that logic and spirit are brought together. Nature is not alien to pure thought, but is the mode of transition from pure logic to its incarnation in spiritual life. This syllogism involves, then, a transitive relationship, rather like that involved in the Barbara syllogism of traditional logic.

The second syllogism has spirit as the mediating agent, in that it presupposes nature and brings out its inherent logic as a result. The move here involves reflection (as in the discussion of essence) and leads to a kind of subjective cognition that in turn aims at freedom. By examining particulars to discern their universal logical significance, this syllogism is rather like induction.

The third syllogism is, says Hegel, the "idea of philosophy." Reasoning that knows itself, or pure logic, mediates as absolutely universal by distinguishing within itself both spiritual and natural moments—spirit as the presupposed subjective activity of pure thought, and nature as the objective process of reason that exists on its own. Here logic divides itself into the two realms where reason becomes manifest.

Hegel's final sentence is of interest: "And the self-discrimination comes together in the two manifestations of spirit and nature, so that it is the nature of things—the concept—that moves forward and develops. This movement is equally as much the activity of cognition: as absolute spirit, the eternal idea in and of itself keeps itself busy, continually regenerates itself and enjoys itself eternally."[2] Here, again, we have the suggestion that philosophy moves forward as activity and does not simply rest on its laurels.

There has been much discussion on the significance of these three syllogisms. Does it refer to the system, so that the first syllogism describes the *Encyclopaedia* which moves from logic through nature to spirit, the second picks up on the *Phenomenology* where reflective thought looks at its experience of the world to discern its implicit principles, while the third is the work of the *Science of Logic*, in capturing the essence of philosophy?

Or is the system only contained in the final syllogism, where pure thought understands how it divides itself into nature and spirit? (Hegel says, after all, that this inference is the "idea of philosophy.") In that case the first syllogism describes how the world developed from an implicit rationality by way of a created natural order to produce our spiritual capacity to integrate thought and world; and the second describes the way we humans have in fact tried to come to terms with the world by finding its inherent logic—the enterprise of science.

A third reading is also possible. For one could see this as the pattern of all life: that thought and intention acts to produce something objective with all its contingencies which becomes in turn a component of spiritual life; that reflection always takes what has happened in the world and looks for its rational significance; and that thought then recognizes how the contingencies of the natural order that emerge from all action and the subjective integrations of spirit are all parts of its own internal dynamic. These three syllogisms not only summarize the basic structure of Hegel's whole philosophical system, but also tell us how things will develop from here. They capture in a nutshell what Hegel means by "spirit absolute."

---

2. G.W.F. Hegel, *Philosophy of Mind*, tr. W. Wallace & A.V. Miller, (Oxford: Oxford University Press, 1971) §577; GW: 20, 571. This paragraph has been extensively rewritten from the earlier 1817 version.

PART VII

Afterthought

Chapter 23

After Hegel

Hegel's claim that all rational discourse could ultimately be integrated into a systematic framework caught the imagination of British and American philosophers during the nineteenth century. In 1844 the young Benjamin Jowett travelled from Oxford to Germany where he was introduced to Hegel's thought by Johann Eduard Erdmann.[1] From then on he not only encouraged the study of Hegel among his students at Oxford, but even began a translation of the *Encyclopaedia Logic*.

Then, the unsuccessful revolutions of 1848 in Europe released a flood of young immigrants to the United States, many of whom introduced German thought to that young country. Around 1858 in St. Louis, Missouri, the German émigré, Henry Conrad Brokmeyer converted William Torrey Harris to Hegelianism, and with others they inaugurated a systematic study of Hegel based on Brokmeyer's translation of the larger *Logic*. The result in both countries was a flourishing of neo-Hegelian logics.

For Harris (1835–1909), the "objective dialectic" is a process which results when a thought is assumed to be universally valid and true. Whether a concept is taken simply on its own, as negatively related to its contraries, or as the positive identity of such contraries, logic will lay bare its imperfections and in so doing pass over to a more profound thought—one which contains explicitly what had previously been only implicit. This dialectic, when developed into a system, contains solutions for all the problems posed by experience.[2]

For the Cambridge philosopher, J.M.E. McTaggart (1866–1925) on the other hand, the logic analyses what happens when categories are

1. J.E. Erdmann, *Outlines of Logic and Metaphysics* (1841), tr. B.C. Burt (London: Sonnenschein, 1896), and *A History of Philosophy* (1866), tr. W.S. Hough (London: Sonnenschein, 1890–92).
2. W.T. Harris, *Hegel's Logic: A Book on the Genesis of the Categories of the Mind* (Chicago: Griggs, 1890), and W.T. Harris, *Hegel's Doctrine of Reflection* (New York: Appleton, 1881).

attributed to a subject. Whenever we predicate any concept except the last with any consistency we are forced to apply its contrary to the same subject. The resulting contradiction between the thesis and its antithesis requires a synthesis that reconciles them within a higher category.

This pattern, however, is gradually modified in the course of the logic: in the discussion of essence, the contraries mutually imply each other, and in the logic of concept each category expresses the "truest significance" of its predecessor, so that at this stage the logic develops no opposition or contradiction, and so requires no reconciliation. McTaggart draws the implication that reality, the only subject that can truly be characterized by these logical predicates, is itself continuous and developmental. The early moves through thesis and antithesis to synthesis, then, do not describe reality as it actually is, but rather reflect the way finite and incomplete thought corrects its subjective and limited predications on the way to completeness. Reality or the Absolute, however, is not affected by such negativity.[3]

The study of logic as the way thoughts are predicated of reality is taken up by F.H. Bradley (1846–1924) and Bernard Bosanquet (1848–1923), both educated at Oxford. In his *Principles of Logic*,[4] Bradley argues that one must distinguish purely grammatical forms from the underlying logical relation, in which a judgement as a whole predicates a single complex thought (expressed in the sentence) to reality as the ultimate subject. Thus all judgements are both categorical and hypothetical: hypothetical in that they express the connections between thoughts; categorical in that they affirm reality itself to be connected in this way. The role of inference is to elaborate the systematic interconnections that are true of the self-existent, self-contained and complete Absolute. It can do so, however, because the mediating connections it brings forward depend on "the unbroken individuality of a single subject." Logic, then, both analyses reality into its elements and shows how those elements are synthetically interconnected.

Bosanquet's *Logic or the Morphology of Knowledge* builds on Bradley's theory of judgement, but shows in a more Hegelian way how the various types of judgement and inference can be ordered in a systematic way so that they present a continuous development of forms from simple qualification through comparison, measurement, singular, universal, negative and disjunctive judgements into those inferences which make explicit the necessary ground of any judgement. These, too, have what Bosanquet calls a morphology, in that one can trace how each one grows logically out of

3. J.M.E. McTaggart, *Studies in the Hegelian Dialectic* (Cambridge: Cambridge University Press, 1896), J.M.E. McTaggart, *Studies in Hegelian Cosmology* (Cambridge: Cambridge University Press, 1901), and J.M.E. McTaggart, *A Commentary on Hegel's Logic* (Cambridge: Cambridge University Press, 1910).
4. F.H. Bradley, *The Principles of Logic* (Oxford: Clarendon Press, 1883).

what precedes it. Starting from enumerative induction and mathematical reasoning, he proceeds to analogy, perceptive analysis, hypothesis and finally concrete systematic inference. Since all such reasoning is predicated of reality, it provides the foundation for knowledge. "The comparative value of these forms of knowledge," he writes, "and the affinities between them, are the object-matter of Logical Science."[5]

In British idealism, then, the systematic interrelation of thought which is the focus of Hegel's logic is explicitly metaphysical. Working from several remarks in Hegel's *Encyclopaedia Logic*, they understand logical categories to be predicates of a singular reality (or the Absolute), and the role of logic is to educate the mind to the point where it can grasp this reality as a whole.

The American Charles S. Peirce (1839–1914) initially had contempt for the Hegelianism of his contemporaries, but eventually allowed that his philosophy resuscitated Hegel in a strange costume. Peirce's three categories were anticipated in Hegel's being, essence and concept. Indeed, "it appears to me that Hegel is so nearly right that my own doctrine might very well be taken for a variety of Hegelianism."[6] Hegel erred, however, in incorporating fact, and to a lesser extent quality, into the interconnections of thought, so that "the element of Secondness, of *hard fact*, is not accorded its true place in his system."[7] In a sense, what Peirce missed was a critical aspect of that negativity and finitude which McTaggart, as well as the other idealists who equated reality with a single individual absolute, had wanted to discount because of its partiality.

The interpretation of Hegel's logic offered in this book is based on the conviction that Hegel does in fact take "secondness" seriously. His *Phenomenology of Spirit* traces the development of human experience as it learns from the failure of its confident claims to knowledge once they have been put into practice. Secondness confounds expectations. It reaches its culmination when it can show that the self-determining life of spirit—that is, of humans both individually and as cultural communities—knows by putting its convictions into practice and learning from both the successes and the failures of those ventures. Human reasoning is nothing else but this dynamic of lived experience as it has been distilled into the essence of thought. Thought, then, is the way humans conceive not only the world they experience but also their own intellectual activity. The simple dialectical

---

5. Bernard Bosanquet, *Logic or the Morphology of Knowledge* (Oxford: Clarendon Press, 1888), Vol II, p. 236.
6. *The Collected Papers of Charles Sanders Peirce*, edited by Charles Hartshorne and Paul Weiss (Cambridge, MA: Harvard University Press, 1931–35) Vol 5, paragraph 5.38. The passage was written in 1903.
7. *Collected Papers*, Vol 1, paragraph 524, again written in 1903.

transitions, the reflective syntheses and the conceptual unities of Hegel's logic are just the way intelligent life determines itself as thought.[8]

This reading, however, is only one among many. A selection from English-speaking Hegel interpreters during the twentieth century will suggest some of the alternatives.

For many years the only available commentary after McTaggart's was that of G.R.G. Mure,[9] an heir of the nineteenth century British idealists. For Mure the Absolute is active spirit, and the philosopher as a participant in its life thinks its categories as they apply in perception (the logic of being), in empirical explanation (the logic of essence) and in philosophical thinking itself. The moves from thought to thought are not explained by the inherent character of each category *per se*, but by the fact that all are grounded in the persisting presence of spirit, yet separated out as singular thoughts.

For Errol E. Harris,[10] the Absolute is simply to be understood as the whole, and speculative thought is that which thinks this reality as a whole. The teleological drive to completeness thus "sublates" or overcomes the finitude of each limited concept by forcing its implicit antithesis to become explicit so that both contraries can be incorporated into their synthesis.

Charles Taylor,[11] avoiding the language of the Absolute, suggests that for Hegel the categories apply to reality in general. Each one is indispensable as a way spirit posits the things to which concepts apply. But because such limited terms do not satisfy the standard of coherence which any conception of reality must meet, they show themselves to be incoherent, requiring more adequate terms.

For Clark Butler,[12] the categories of the *Logic* are, however, predicates of the Absolute, and the logic develops as each predicate is taken in isolation, found to be incoherent and so fails, requiring a more comprehensive description. He distinguishes nine distinct steps within this process of indirect proof.

Mure, E. Harris, Taylor and Butler all assume that the categories of Hegel's logic function as predicates of a subject which is none other than reality as such—the Absolute or the whole. For them, the logic is essentially

8. Compare John Burbidge, *On Hegel's Logic: Fragments of a Commentary* (Atlantic Highlands, NJ: Humanities, 1981), John Burbidge, *Hegel on Logic and Religion: The Reasonableness of Christianity* (Albany, NY: State University of New York Press, 1992) and *Real Process: How Logic and Chemistry combine in Hegel's Philosophy of Nature* (Toronto: University of Toronto Press, 1996).

9. G.R.G. Mure, *A Study of Hegel's Logic* (Oxford: Clarendon Press, 1950).

10. E.E. Harris, *An Interpretation of the Logic of Hegel* (Lanham, MD: University Press of America, 1983).

11. Charles Taylor, *Hegel* (Cambridge: Cambridge University Press, 1975).

12. Clark Butler, *Hegel's Logic: Between Dialectic and History* (Evanston, IL: Northwestern University Press, 1997).

a metaphysics. Stephen Houlgate[13] maintains a metaphysical reading, but of a different order. For Houlgate, the logic works without foundations, and so cannot presuppose reality as the subject of which the categories are predicated. Rather, thinking is itself being. As a result, the logic conducts an immanent critique of the traditional concepts of metaphysics and, by showing their true character, yields a determinate philosophical knowledge of reality. The truth of this systematic construction becomes manifest when its conclusions accord with common experience.[14]

Robert Pippin,[15] however, rejects any metaphysical reading of the *Logic*. For Pippin, Hegel is following a Kantian project—of articulating those concepts that we require whenever we think in a rigorous way about any possible object whatsoever and then explore their categorical commitments. This requires an exposition not only of those terms that refer to objects, but also of those that apply to the self-conscious judge of objects. Since Hegel, following Fichte, rejects Kant's claim that concepts on their own are empty and must be completed with reference to sensible intuitions by way of the schematism, he has to justify their transcendental use through the internal connections that are shown to hold between categories and so reflect the self-determining power of pure thought. While the British idealists had argued that the coherence of thought reflected the coherence of reality, Pippin makes a more modest claim: it is the systematic, or holistic "dialectical" interrelatedness of these determinations of possible objects which legitimates the transcendental use of the categories.

Terry Pinkard, in *Hegel's Dialectic: The Explanation of Possibility*, adopts a similar, non-metaphysical reading. Concepts for Hegel are defined by the rules according to which they can be used, and the role of logic is to reconstruct and reorder the categories so that they become compatible. This systematic redescription starts with simple determinations, moves on to the relation of substructure to superstructure and concludes with an examination of the principles used in the very act of conceiving.[16]

In his later *Hegel: A Biography*, however, Pinkard reverts to a metaphysical reading, claiming that Hegel had taken over from his friend, the poet Hölderlin, the conviction that thought and being are one, so that the logic starts with judgements we make about finite entities that come to be and pass away, moves on to the relation between appearance and reality, and

---

13. Stephen Houlgate, *Hegel, Nietzsche and the Criticism of Metaphysics* (Cambridge: Cambridge University Press, 1986), and Stephen Houlgate, *Freedom, Truth and History: An Introduction to Hegel's Philosophy* (London: Routledge, 1991).

14. If such a correspondence fails to appear, says Houlgate, it reflects either a flaw in the logical explanation or an improper application to experience.

15. Robert B. Pippin, *Hegel's Idealism: The Satisfactions of Self-consciousness* (Cambridge: Cambridge University Press, 1989).

16. Terry Pinkard, *Hegel's Dialectic: The Explanation of Possibility* (Philadelphia: Temple University Press, 1988).

concludes with the "normative structure" of social space. The *Logic* thus equates being to the rationality of modern humanity.[17]

Some (for example Dominique Dubarle and André Doz[18]) have tried to formalize Hegel's logic, but their proposals have not won general acceptance, since they require the introduction of non-formal conditions to generate Hegel's logical transitions.

There are, then, various ways of reading the *Logic* of Hegel. The metaphysical approach itself ranges from those who see the categories as predicates of a single entity incorporating all reality that can be called the Absolute, to those who claim that the logic just articulates those connections between determinate concepts that we have found necessary in our experience. In either case, it is reality itself that requires the move from concept to concept. On the other hand, the logical readings claim that each concept has its own network of meaning that requires reference to other meanings, some of which conflict, requiring a conceptual resolution of the paradox.

Hegel's text is rich enough to carry both interpretations and suggest many more. One should never rest with accepted traditions, but go back continually to the original (preferably in the German since "all translations traduce"[19] as the Italians say), study it carefully and struggle with finding a way of incorporating all its abstract terminology into a coherent argument. As that is done new readings will emerge.

17. Terry Pinkard, *Hegel: A Biography* (Cambridge: Cambridge University Press, 2000).

18. Dominique Dubarle and André Doz, *Logique et Dialectique* (Paris: Larousse, 1972).

19. "Traduce" equals "calumniate," or "misrepresent" (*Oxford Concise Dictionary*, 1982).

Chapter 24

Conclusion

Hegel's *Science of Logic* is certainly not a logic in the conventional sense. Yet in this book I have argued that he is nonetheless investigating the processes of thought that underlie logical thinking—those processes that find expression not only in formal syllogisms but in all reasoning from some meaningful concepts to others. Our thought moves directly from one conception to another in what can be called "immediate transitions"; it reflects back over a set of such moves as a whole, bringing them together into a synthesis to discover their ground or explanation; and, says Hegel following Kant, it integrates or unites these double transitions, together with their starting and concluding terms, into new concepts. These are sufficiently self-contained that they can be in their turn isolated and considered on their own, apart from the mediating process that led up to them.

One could set out these three moves—dialectic, speculation and understanding—in a formal schema, and simply apply it in a mechanical way to any content whatsoever. Hegel, however, rejects such a move. For the initial transitions follow only from the specific meaning of the concept we are trying to understand. The resulting thought is thus not an external opposite, but implicitly contained somehow in the sense of the notion from where we started. Similarly, the reflective synthesis does not just impose on our thoughts some kind of subjective predisposition to see connections, but rather highlights and identifies those particular implications that triggered the immediate inference. Finally, the unity that constitutes the new integrated concept must be justified with sufficient reason—that is, it must show that it follows from the specific content being thought.

Since formal patterns cannot do justice to logical thinking Hegel cannot provide a neat summary of his method.[1] The logical ground of all reasoning is not found in the formal relationship of terms, propositions and syllogisms, but in the meanings of concepts—the way they are defined relative to other terms and incorporate specific components in specific ways. Once we begin to examine thought from this perspective, we find that the concepts we think are not a simple collection of diverse terms; they develop one from another. We can start from the most simple and indeterminate thought and move on to the most complex and comprehensive. This developmental framework, Hegel claims, underlies the assumptions, inferences and judgements of reasonability that permeate all intellectual discourse. Understanding the nature of this development will not only affect the way we think; it will also improve our ability to communicate with other thinking beings.

If Hegel's logic is read as simply developing an arbitrary system peculiar to himself, it can be dismissed as an interesting curiosity. On the other hand, if it is read as articulating the structure of all human thinking, it opens for us the possibility of satisfying the Delphic injunction: we may come to know ourselves. For even when we are furthest removed from the realm of abstract thought—when we are reacting with anger to an affront, or immersed in the beauty of a sunset—it is the meaning of what is happening that has enveloped us. Our response is seldom if ever simply instinctive. We read what occurs as significant; and our reaction draws out its implications. So if we are to move beyond simply being the prey to the changing fashions of our feelings, if we are to become free in the sense that we can decide for ourselves how we should react, then we must bring those implicit relationships of meaning to the fore and come to understand how they work and where they lead.

Hegel, of course, wants to go further. The structures of reason are not simply the peculiar characteristics of an aberrant species. They are inherent in the cosmos itself. His *Phenomenology* shows us how we learn the habits of reason through our experience. We discover that our beliefs and expectations are misguided, and so are led to revise them until we no longer are surprised. The success of science and technology in exploring our natural and social world confirms that our reasoning and the inherent structures of reality can be made to conform to each other. We are not simply imposing our thought on a recalcitrant matter. Matter itself is potentially reasonable. And over time we have discovered how this rationality fits in with our thinking. This is why Hegel says that we can set even the work of science within a comprehensive logical framework, which he calls the Philosophy of Nature and the Philosophy of Spirit.

---

1. Though one could say that the Paragraphs 79 to 82 in the *Encyclopaedia Logic* on understanding, dialectic and speculative reason do offer such a summary. Compare what Hegel says about method in the Introduction to the larger *Logic: GW* 21, 38–41; *SL* 54–57.

For all that success, however, we continually discover new truths. What has been accepted as unquestionable has proven to be unreliable. Projects we have carefully designed based on past experience have turned out to be failures. In the reading of the *Phenomenology* presented here, Hegel claims that this is inherent in all knowing. We come to expect that, for all of our successes, we will always be surprised. It is with this very dynamic of encountering failure that we learn how the transitions of dialectical reason into the opposite of where we began are incorporated into the structure of the cosmos.

Hegel is not the first to affirm that humans are able to establish contact with the ultimate sense of the universe. This belief is at the core of all science, of all religion, of all philosophy. It finds expression as well in the genius of the artist and the beauty of the work of art. So we can learn, not only from the discoveries made by the natural sciences, but also by coming to appreciate the way humans over the ages have made sense of their world. By extending our perspective to the whole gamut of human history we overcome our biases and bring to light dimensions of our rationality that have been suppressed and forgotten. The success, limited though it may be, of all such ventures at self-knowledge only serves to confirm Hegel's conviction that the cosmos itself is rational.

Whether the details of Hegel's philosophy have, in fact, captured what it means to be human is a question that must be left unanswered. Even he was prepared to rework his lectures in the light of second thoughts and new evidence. Nonetheless there remains his fundamental conception: our human thinking is inherently rational; this rationality has emerged from the workings of the cosmos and, in particular, from the whole gamut of human experience; and with disciplined thought we can bring all of this to the surface, and come to understand how it works.

If, once that is done, we react from boredom or anger, convinced that there is something more, we are simply reaffirming the basic pattern of all rationality. The unacceptable meaning of what we are given triggers a reaction to produce something different. That leads, in due course, to some attempt at a synthesis, and, possibly, an ultimate integration into a new reality. Once that becomes familiar and traditional the whole process will start again, continuing to prove that not only is the rational actual, but the actual is also rational.

Further Reading

German Editions of Hegel's Works

Hegel, G.W.F. *Gesammelte Werke.* [*GW*] Edition commissioned by the Deutschen Forschungsgemeinshaft. Hamburg: Meiner, 1968–.
Hegel, G.W.F. *Vorlesungen: Ausgewählte Nachschriften und Manuskripte.* [V] Hamburg: Meiner, 1983–.

These are the German editions referred to in this book. There are, however, several cheap student editions of Hegel's writing available:

Hegel, G.W.F. *Werke.* Edited by E. Moldenhauer and K.M. Michel. Frankfurt am Main: Suhrkamp, 1970.

Based on the *Werke* produced by Hegel's disciples in 1832–1845. It includes the lecture material based on student notes.

Over the years the *Philosophischen Bibliothek* published by Felix Meiner in Hamburg has included most, if not all, of Hegel's works. Originally these were edited by Georg Lasson (later Johannes Hoffmeister and others), and included material that had previously only been available in manuscript. More recently Meiner has used texts from the Critical Edition above.

English Translations of Hegel's Works

I am citing only first editions. Many have been reprinted.

Early Theological Writings. Translated by T.M. Knox and R. Kroner. Chicago: University of Chicago Press, 1948.
The Jena System, 1804–5: Logic and Metaphysics. Translated by J.W. Burbidge, G. di Giovanni, H.S. Harris et al. Montreal: McGill-Queen's University Press, 1986.

There are a number of other translations of manuscripts and published writing prior to the *Phenomenology*. These two are mentioned in particular because I have referred to them in the text.

The Phenomenology of Mind. Translated by J.B. Baillie. London: Sonnenschein, 1910.
Hegel's Phenomenology of Spirit. Translated by A.V. Miller. Oxford: Oxford University Press, 1977.
Hegel's Science of Logic. Translated by W.H. Johnston and L.G. Struthers. London: George Allen & Unwin, 1929.

Hegel's Science of Logic. [SL] Translated by A.V. Miller. London: George Allen & Unwin, 1969.

Encyclopedia of the Philosophical Sciences in Outline and Critical Writings. [1817 edition] Translated by S.A. Taubeneck and others. New York: Continuum, 1990.

The Encyclopaedia Logic. [1830] *[EL]* Translated by T.F. Geraets, W.A. Suchting, H.S. Harris. Indianapolis, ID: Hackett, 1991.

The Logic of Hegel. [1830] Translated by W. Wallace. Oxford: Oxford University Press, 1874.

The Encyclopaedia Logic with additions.
Indiana University Press in Bloomington is publishing a translation by Clark Butler of Karl Hegel's notes from Hegel's *Lectures on Logic* of 1831.

Hegel's Philosophy of Nature. [1830] Translated by M.J. Petry. London: Allen & Unwin, 1970.

The notes in this edition provide valuable material on the natural science of Hegel's day.

Hegel's Philosophy of Nature. [1830] Translated by A.V. Miller. Oxford: Oxford University Press, 1970.

Philosophy of Subjective Spirit. [1830 with the 1822 and 1825 lectures] Translated by M.J. Petry. Dordrecht: Reidel, 1981.

Like Petry's edition of the *Philosophy of Nature*, this has extensive notes citing contemporary literature in Anthropology and Psychology.

Hegel's Philosophy of Mind. [1830] Translated by W. Wallace with the Additions translated by A.V. Miller. Oxford: Oxford University Press, 1971.

Hegel's Philosophy of Right. Translated by S.W. Dyde. London: Bell, 1896.

Hegel's Philosophy of Right. Translated by T.M. Knox. Oxford: Oxford University Press, 1942.

Hegel's Philosophy of Right. Translated by H.B. Nisbett. Cambridge: Cambridge University Press, 1991.

Lectures on the Philosophy of History. [Karl Hegel edition of 1840] Translated by J. Sibree. London: Bohn, 1857.

There have been a number of more recent translations of the introduction to this edition. The following, however, is based on the introduction as edited by Johannes Hoffmeister:

Lectures on the Philosophy of World History: Introduction. [Hoffmeister edition of 1955] Translated by H.B. Nisbett. Cambridge: Cambridge University Press, 1975.

Hegel's Aesthetics: Lectures on Fine Art. Translated by T.M. Knox. Oxford: Oxford University Press, 1975.

Lectures on the Philosophy of Religion. [Marheineke edition of 1840] Translated by E.B. Speirs & J.B. Sanderson. London: Paul, Tench, 1885.

Lectures on the Philosophy of Religion. [W. Jaeschke edition of 1983–5 in *V*] Translated by P.C. Hodgson, R.F. Brown, J.M. Stewart. Berkeley: University of California Press, 1984–7.

Lectures on the History of Philosophy. [Michelet edition of 1840] Translated by E.S. Haldane & F.H. Simpson. London: Paul, Tench, 1892–99.

Lectures on the History of Philosophy: The Lectures of 1825–26. [Garniron & Jaeschke edition of 1986–96] Translated by R.F. Brown & J.M. Stewart. Berkeley: University of California Press, 1990–.

Cambridge University Press has commissioned a new set of translations of the major texts that is now being prepared.

Hegel: The Letters. Translated by C. Butler & C. Seiler. Bloomington: Indiana University Press, 1984.

Secondary Sources

Books in English on Hegel's Thought in General

Beiser, Frederick. *Hegel.* London: Routledge, 2005.
Berthold-Bond, Daniel. *Hegel's Grand Synthesis.* Albany: State University of New York Press, 1989.
Burbidge, J.W. *Historical Dictionary of Hegelian Philosophy.* Lanham, MD: Scarecrow, 2001.
Butler, Clark. *G.W.F. Hegel.* Boston: Twayne, 1977.
Caird, Edward. *Hegel.* Edinburgh: Blackwood, 1883.

Still one of the best introductions to Hegel available.

The Cambridge Companion to Hegel. Edited by F.C. Beiser. Cambridge: Cambridge University Press, 1993.
Findlay, John N. *Hegel: A Re-examination.* London: Allen & Unwin, 1958.
Houlgate, Stephen. *Freedom, Truth and History: An Introduction to Hegel's Philosophy.* London: Routledge, 1991.
Inwood, Michael. *Hegel.* London: Routledge & Kegan Paul, 1983.
—. *A Hegel Dictionary.* Oxford: Blackwell, 1992.
Kainz, Howard. *G.W.F. Hegel: The Philosophical System.* New York: Twayne, 1996.
Kaufmann, Walter. *Hegel: Reinterpretation, Texts and Commentary.* Garden City, NJ: Doubleday, 1965.
Kojève, Alexandre. *Introduction to the Reading of Hegel.* Edited by A. Bloom; translated by J.H. Nichols. New York: Basic Books, 1969.
Mure, G.R.G. *An Introduction to Hegel.* Oxford: Oxford University Press, 1940.
—. *The Philosophy of Hegel.* London: Oxford University Press, 1965.
Pippin, Robert B. *Hegel's Idealism: The Satisfactions of Self-consciousness.* Cambridge: Cambridge University Press, 1989.
Plant, Raymond. *Hegel: An Introduction.* London: Allen & Unwin, 1973.
Rose, Gillian. *Hegel Contra Sociology.* London: Athlone, 1981.
Rosen, Stanley. *G.W.F. Hegel: An Introduction to the Science of Wisdom.* New Haven, CT: Yale University Press, 1974.
Singer, Peter. *Hegel: A very short Introduction.* Oxford: Oxford University Press, 1983.
Soll, Ivan. *An Introduction to Hegel's Metaphysics.* Chicago: University of Chicago Press, 1969.
Stace, Walter T. *The Philosophy of Hegel: A Systematic Exposition.* London: Macmillan, 1924.
Stirling, J. Hutchison. *The Secret of Hegel: Being the Hegelian System in Origin, Principle, Form and Matter.* London: Longman, Roberts & Green, 1865.
Taylor, Charles. *Hegel.* Cambridge: Cambridge University Press, 1975.

Books and Articles in English on Hegel's Logic

Ahlers, Rolf. "The Absolute as the Beginning of Hegel's Logic." *The Philosophical Forum* 6 (1974–5): 288–300.

Art and Logic in Hegel's Philosophy. Edited by Warren E. Steinkraus and Kenneth Schmitz. Atlantic Highlands, NJ: Humanities, 1980.

Baillie, James B. *The Origin and Significance of Hegel's Logic*. London: Macmillan, 1901.

Baur, Michael. "Sublating Kant and the Old Metaphysics: A Reading of the Transition from Being to Essence in Hegel's *Logic*." *The Owl of Minerva* 29, no. 2 (Spring 1998): 139–164.

Burbidge, John W. *Hegel on Logic and Religion*. Albany, NY: State University of New York Press, 1992.

—. *On Hegel's Logic: Fragments of a Commentary*. Atlantic Highlands, NJ: Humanities, 1981.

Butler, Clark. *Hegel's Logic: Between Dialectic and History*. Evanston, IL: Northwestern University Press, 1997.

Cave, George P. "The Dialectic of Becoming in Hegel's Logic." *The Owl of Minerva* 16, no. 2 (Spring 1985): 147–160.

Cooper, Rebecca. *The Logical Influence of Hegel on Marx*. Seattle: University of Washington Press, 1925.

Dahlstrom, Daniel O. "Hegel's Science of Logic and Idea of Truth." *Idealistic Studies* 13 (1983): 33–49.

di Giovanni, George. "Reflection and Contradiction: A Commentary on some Passages of Hegel's Science of Logic." *Hegel-Studien* 8 (1973): 131–62.

Essays on Hegel's Logic. Edited by George di Giovanni. Albany, N.Y.: State University of New York Press, 1990.

Ferrini, Cinzia. "On the Relation between 'Mode' and 'Measure' in Hegel's *Science of Logic*: Some Introductory Remarks." *The Owl of Minerva* 20, no. 1 (Fall 1988): 21–49.

Harris, Errol E. *An Interpretation of the Logic of Hegel*. Lanham, MD: University Press of America, 1983.

Harris, William T. *Hegel's Doctrine of Reflection*. New York: Appleton, 1881.

—. *Hegel's Logic: A Book on the Genesis of the Categories of the Mind*. Chicago: Griggs, 1890.

Hartnack, Justus. *Hegel's Logic*. (1995) Translated by Lars Aagaard-Mogensen. Indianapolis, IN: Hackett, 1998.

Hibben, John G. *Hegel's Logic: An Essay in Interpretation*. New York: Scribner, 1902.

Hoffmeyer, John F. *The Advent of Freedom: The Presence of the Future in Hegel's Logic*. Cranbury, NJ: Associated Universities Press, 1994.

Houlgate, Stephen. "Necessity and Contingency in Hegel's *Science of Logic*." *The Owl of Minerva* 27 no. 1 (Fall 1995): 37–49.

—. "Hegel's Critique of Foundationalism in the 'Doctrine of Essence'." *Bulletin of the Hegel Society of Great Britain* 39/40 (1999): 18–34.

Hyppolite, Jean. *Logic and Existence*. (1932) Translated by Leonard Lawlor and Amit Sen. Albany, NY: State University of New York Press, 1997.

Johnson, Paul. *The Critique of Thought: A Re-examination of Hegel's Science of Logic*. Aldershot, England: Gower, 1988.

Lachterman, David. "Hegel and the Formalization of Logic." *Graduate Faculty Journal* 12, nos 1–2 (1980): 153–89.

Macran, H.S. *Hegel's Doctrine of Formal Logic: Being a translation of the first section of the Subjective Logic*. Oxford: Clarendon, 1912.

Marcuse, Herbert. *Hegel's Ontology and the Theory of Historicity*. (1932) Translated by Seyla Benhabib. Cambridge, MA: MIT Press, 1987.

McCumber, John. *The Company of Words: Hegel, Language and Systematic Philosophy.* Evanston, IL.: Northwestern University Press, 1993.

McTaggart, John M.E. *A Commentary on Hegel's Logic.* Cambridge: Cambridge University Press, 1910.

—. *Studies in Hegelian Dialectic.* Cambridge: Cambridge University Press, 1896.

Mueller, Gustav E. "The Hegelian Legend of 'Thesis-Antithesis-Synthesis'." *The Journal of the History of Ideas* 19 (1958): 411–14.

Mure, G.R.G. *A Study of Hegel's Logic.* Oxford: Clarendon, 1950.

Pinkard, Terry. *Hegel's Dialectic: The Explanation of Possibility.* Philadelphia: Temple University Press, 1988.

Rockmore, Tom. "Foundationalism and Hegelian Logic." *The Owl of Minerva* 21, no. 1 (Fall 1989): 41–50.

Rosen, Michael. *Hegel's Dialectic and its Criticism.* Cambridge: Cambridge University Press, 1982.

Rowe, William V. "Essence, Ground and First Philosophy in Hegel's *Science of Logic*." *The Owl of Minerva* 18, no. 1 (Fall 1986): 43–56.

Sarlemijn, Andries. *Hegel's Dialectic.* (1971) Translated by P. Kirschenmann. Dordrecht: Reidel, 1975.

Schmitz, Kenneth L. "Hegel's Attempt to Forge a Logic for Spirit." *Dialogue* 10 (1971): 653–72.

Wallace, William. *Prolegomena to the Study of Hegel's Philosophy and especially of his Logic.* Oxford: Clarendon, 1894.

White, Alan. *Absolute Knowledge: Hegel and the Problem of Metaphysics.* Athens, OH: Ohio University Press, 1983.

Books in English on other Works by Hegel

Avinieri, Shlomo. *Hegel's Theory of the Modern State.* Cambridge: Cambridge University Press, 1972.

Burbidge, J. *Real Process: How Logic and Chemistry Combine in Hegel's Philosophy of Nature.* Toronto: University of Toronto Press, 1996.

Cullen, Bernard. *Hegel's Social and Political Thought: An Introduction.* Dublin: Gill & Macmillan, 1979.

Desmond, William. *Art and the Absolute: A Study of Hegel's Aesthetics.* Albany: State University of New York Press, 1986.

De Vries, Willem. *Hegel's Theory of Mental Activity.* Ithaca, NY: Cornell University Press, 1988.

Fackenheim, Emil L. *The Religious Dimension of Hegel's Thought.* Bloomington: Indiana University Press, 1967.

Flay, Joseph. *Hegel's Quest for Certainty.* Albany: State University of New York Press, 1984.

Greene, Murray. *Hegel on the Soul: A Speculative Anthropology.* The Hague: Nijhoff, 1972.

Harris, H.S. *Hegel's Development. Volume I: Toward the Sunlight 1770–1801.* Oxford: Oxford University Press, 1972.

—. *Hegel's Development. Volume II: Night Thoughts. Jena 1801–1806.* Oxford: Oxford University Press, 1983.

—. *Hegel's Ladder I: The Pilgrimage of Reason; II: The Odyssey of Spirit.* Indianapolis IN: Hackett, 1997.

Hegel and the Philosophy of Nature. Edited by Stephen Houlgate. Albany: State University of New York Press, 1998.

Hyppolite, Jean. *Genesis and Structure of Hegel's Phenomenology of Spirit.* Translated by Samuel Cherniak and John Heckman. Evanston, IL: Northwestern University Press, 1974.

Jaeschke, Walter. *Reason in Religion.* Translated by J. Michael Stewart and Peter C. Hodgson. Berkeley: University of California Press, 1990.

Kainz, Howard P. *Hegel's Phenomenology, Part I: Analysis and Commentary.* Tuscaloosa: University of Alabama Press, 1976.

—. *Hegel's Phenomenology, Part II: The Evolution of Ethical and Religious Consciousness to the Dialectical Standpoint.* Athens: Ohio University Press, 1983.

Kaminsky, Jack. *Hegel on Art: An Interpretation of Hegel's Aesthetics.* Albany: State University of New York Press, 1962.

Kelly, George. *Hegel's Retreat from Eleusis: Studies in Political Thought.* Princeton, NJ: Princeton University Press, 1978.

Lakeland, Paul. *The Politics of Salvation: The Hegelian Idea of the State.* Albany: State University of New York Press, 1989.

Norman, Richard. *Hegel's Phenomenology: A Philosophical Introduction.* London: Sussex University Press, 1976.

O'Brien, G.D. *Hegel on Reason and History.* Chicago: Chicago University Press, 1975.

Peperzak, Adriaan. *Philosophy and Politics: A Commentary on the Preface to Hegel's Philosophy of Right.* The Hague: Nijhoff, 1987.

Pinkard, Terry. *Hegel's Phenomenology: The Sociality of Reason.* Cambridge: Cambridge University Press, 1994.

Rockmore, Tom. *Cognition: An Introduction to Hegel's Phenomenology of Spirit.* Berkeley: University of California Press, 1997.

Solomon, Robert. *In the Spirit of Hegel: A Study of Hegel's Phenomenology of Spirit.* Oxford: Oxford University Press, 1983.

Verene, Donald. *Hegel's Recollection: A Study of Images in the Phenomenology of Spirit.* Albany: State University of New York Press, 1985.

Walsh, W.H. *Hegelian Ethics.* London: Macmillan, 1969.

Weil, Eric. *Hegel and the State.* Translated by Mark A. Cohen. Baltimore, MD: Johns Hopkins University Press, 1998.

Westphal, Kenneth. *Hegel's Epistemological Realism: A Study of the Aim and Method of Hegel's Phenomenology of Spirit.* Dordrecht: Kluwer, 1989.

Westphal, Merold. *History and Truth in Hegel's Phenomenology.* Atlantic Highlands, NJ: Humanities, 1979.

Wilkins, B.T. *Hegel's Philosophy of History.* Ithaca, NY: Cornell University Press, 1974.

Williamson, Raymond K. *Introduction to Hegel's Philosophy of Religion.* Albany: State University of New York Press, 1984.

Hegelian Logics

Adorno, Theodor W. *Negative Dialectics.* Translated by E.B. Ashton. New York: Seabury, 1973.

Bosanquet, Bernard. *Logic or the Morphology of Knowledge.* Oxford: Clarendon, 1888.

Bradley, Francis H. *The Principles of Logic.* Oxford: Clarendon Press, 1883.

Dewey, John. *Logic: The Theory of Inquiry.* New York: Holt, 1938.

Erdmann, Johann Eduard. *Outline of Logic and Metaphysics* [Originally published 1841] Translated by B.C. Burt. London: Sonnenschein, 1896.

McTaggart, John M.E. *Studies in Hegelian Cosmology.* Cambridge: Cambridge University Press, 1901.

Index

[Only the chapter titles from Hegel's *Science of Logic* are included in this index. To avoid an overly long list, the names of concepts and categories covered within any of his chapters are omitted, unless important from a more general perspective.]